GUNNISON
AND
SAN JUAN.

A LATE AND RELIABLE DESCRIPTION OF THE
WONDERFUL GOLD AND SILVER BELTS AND IRON
AND COAL FIELDS OF THAT NEWEST AND BEST
LAND FOR PROSPECTOR AND CAPITALIST,

SOUTHWESTERN COLORADO;

WITH FACTS ON CLIMATE, SOIL, FORESTS, SCENERY, GAME, FISH,
CITIES, TOWNS, POPULATION, DEVELOPMENT, ROUTES, RATES OF
FARE, EMPLOYMENT, WAGES, LIVING EXPENSES, ETC.,

AS PRESENTED IN A SERIES OF LETTERS WRITTEN TO THE *NEW YORK WORLD* BY ITS SPECIAL CORRESPONDENT.

ALSO, CONTAINING A VALUABLE APPENDIX ON MINING LAWS.

BY ROBERT E. STRAHORN

New material Copyright © 2012
Western Reflections Publishing Co.
All rights reserved

ISBN 978-1-937851-00-2

Cover and Text Design by Steve Smith, FluiDESIGNS

Printed in the United States

A Historic Reprint Published by
Western Reflections Publishing Company®
P.O. Box 1149
951 N. Highway 149
Lake City, CO 81235
www.westernreflectionspublishing.com

TABLE OF CONTENTS

Publisher's Foreword	Page 2
The Gunnison Country	Page 5
Elk Mountain Mines	Page 15
Crested Butte	Page 30
Gothic and Rock Creek	Page 36
Rocky Mountain Surprises	Page 46
To Prospector and Capitalist	Page 56
San Juan	Page 69
Synopsis of Mining Laws	Page 80
Routes to Gunnison	Page 85
Index	Page 86

PUBLISHER'S FOREWORD

Despite very humble beginnings, Robert Edmund Strahorn became a successful and well-known free-lance newspaper correspondent of the 1870s and 1880s and authored several books on the West. Among other highlights of his life, he was present as a correspondent for *The New York World* and other Eastern newspapers when Crazy Horse surrendered to U.S. troops in 1876. "Strahorn was not just another tenderfoot scribbler from the East, he was a saddle-hardened plainsman – a Westerner from a western family." (Oliver Knight, Robert E. Strahorn, *Propagandist for the West*).

In 1870, at the age of eighteen, Strahorn was advised by a physician to move to the mountains for his health. Following that advice, he became a reporter in Rocky Mountain mining towns such as Denver, Cheyenne, Central City, and Black Hawk; and during that time he made long trips through the mountains looking for material for his many newspaper articles and pamphlets. Strahorn was in Gunnison, Colorado in 1880—a time when the Utes knew they would be removed from their lands as a result of the Meeker Massacre, but had not yet been forced to leave. The removal of the Utes would mean the opening of Western Colorado, a land of rich minerals, lush grasslands, and great promise to American settlers. It was in situations such as this that Strahorn was at his best, and he wrote a glowing report of gold discoveries, railroads, and ranching. Strahorn undoubtedly exaggerated the wealth of the region, but that was his job; something expected of every journalist and newspaper of the time.

Strahorn's rise to fame was meteoric. His book *To the Rockies and Beyond* was noticed by Thomas Kimball, general agent for the Union Pacific Railroad. Kimball showed the book to his boss Jay Gould, who was impressed enough to hire Strahorn to create the Union Pacific Publicity Department. From that department Strahorn flooded the United States with maps, leaflets, folders, books, and monthly newsletters, all touting America's western frontier. One of the best known works put out by the Union Pacific was *New West Illustrated,* a huge photography book showing the wonders of the West. In the 1870s and 1880s Strahorn and his wife Carrie Adell, crisscrossed the American West by railroad, stage, steamboat, on horseback and with pack trains, investigating and reporting on investment opportunities such as those mentioned in this book, and secretly checking out possible extensions for Gould's railroads.

Over time Strahorn wrote about and was identified with many railroad companies, including the Denver and Rio Grande, the Colorado Central, and the Union Pacific Railroads. His works also included the journals of several survey parties, along with guide books and pamphlets encouraging immigration and the purchase of railroad land. He eventually opened and operated the publicity bureaus for the Union Pacific and Kansas Pacific Railroad. His wife, Carrie Green Strahorn, wrote *Fifteen Thousand Miles by Stage*, a very popular book of her time.

Strahorn went on to become a promoter and developer in the Rockies and in the northwestern United States, buying power plants and irrigation companies to support his land projects. However it was reported that to a large extent he had only a paper empire of maps, surveys and proposals. He made and lost at least three fortunes and died a poor man in Spokane, Washington at age 92 in 1944.

"THE NEWEST MARVEL."

"GUNNISON, the newest marvel of that land of marvels, Colorado, is for the first time clearly and intelligently described in today's *World*. This letter is the first of a series which will be written for *The World* by a correspondent whose initials will be a guarantee to readers at all acquainted with the general subject of mining in Colorado both of his competency and impartiality. Leadville itself has not seen so rapid and bewildering a transition from a wilderness to a city as that which in the lapse of much less than twelve months has been witnessed at Gunnison. And the special feature of these impromptu settlements is that they are made to last, and are indeed not for a day but for all time." *New York World* Editorial, Sept. 7, 1880.

THE GUNNISON COUNTRY.

FIRST LETTER: HISTORY, TOPOGRAPHY AND A GLANCE AT PRESENT DEVELOPMENTS.

GUNNISON, COLORADO, Aug. 25, 1880.
The Gunnison country may well be termed "our newest West." This, too, in face of the fact that its entire eastern boundary lies within twenty miles of districts which have been important producers of the precious metals for from twelve to twenty years. Next door to civilization, easy of access, fairly safe and open to development as it now is, and promising to be the El Dorado of 1881, it deserves such fragments of history as we can at this period gather. In the early days of Rocky Mountain exploration this whole region was vaguely defined as "the Grand River Country," its noblest stream, now called Gunnison, being then known as the South Fork of the Grand. Our earliest tangible knowledge of the geography and probable utility comes from Governor Wm. Gilpin, who in 1845, a mere stripling, returned from Oregon to St. Louis, crossing its entire length from west to east. Crossing Southern Utah by one of the old Spanish trails, his course then lay through the valleys of the South Fork of the Grand and Uncompaghre rivers, thence over Cochetopa Pass, at the southeastern rim of the Gunnison country, and thence to Bent's old fort on the Arkansas. He was enthusiastic in his description of the valleys and the country generally, and although pursued at intervals for 100 miles by savages, embodied his knowledge in a map which is now on exhibition at the Executive office, Denver.
The interval between 1845 and 1853 only records vague stories from trappers and Mormons, the former boasting of the

region as an ideal game-field and of the riches in certain almost inaccessible gulches, and the latter taking care to let the world know only what dangers were threatened by savages. This last claim was well supported, or the Mormon crime speciously covered, when in 1853 Captain Gunnison's name was given the region at the expense of his life. While exploring in this vicinity that year for a Pacific railroad route he was killed; history says by Indians, but subsequent developments point to the Mormons as the murderers. In 1854 the indomitable old "Pathfinder," General Fremont, passed over nearly the same country from east to west, but even his glowing tributes to the beauty and richness of the region did not serve to bridge the seven-year gap which ensued with tales of genuine pioneering.

THE WASHINGTON GULCH MASSACRE.

Not until 1861, when some prospectors who approached from California Gulch (where Leadville now stands) and named Washington Gulch, Taylor Park, Rentz's Gulch and Union Park, near the head of Slate River, was there any positive development. Such discoveries as they made created considerable excitement, and under ordinary circumstances would have led to a genuine stampede and permanent occupation of the country, but one morning of the summer named, twelve men who were riding along the Washington Gulch trail were killed by Indians. This wholesale massacre, which gave the gloomy side defile the name of Dead Man's Gulch, sent a thrill of terror through every incoming prospector. The outrage was magnified each time its story was repeated, and the result was an almost entire abandonment of the country by the whites. Not even the stories of "pound diggings," of golden bullets that the Indians used, and of the famous "Snow-Blind Gulch" along the Cochetopa where it was currently believed two miners whip-sawed boards for flumes and washed out a pound of gold each per day, and finally, when the snows of 1862 fell, becoming snow-blind they perished an easy prey to savages or storm, not even these lured the most daring in the then populous gulches of Central Colorado to exploration. I have had "Snow-Blind Gulch" pointed out to me near the headwaters of the Tomichi, with its traces of mining in the long ago—the old whip-saw pit, the rotten sluices and overgrown prospect holes. There are no "pound diggings" or golden bullets there, but gold in the quartz of neighboring hills in paying quantities. I am happy to be able to state also, that the two miners who whip-sawed those boards on the headwaters of the Tomichi did not leave their skeletons there, and I must therefore spoil the tragical feature of this story. The gentlemen are still alive, and are known as two of the best prospectors and miners in the State, James W. Taylor and John Hack.

Taylor River and Taylor Park in the Gunnison, and Taylor's Gulch in the Monarch district are named after the former. Neither of these indomitable men have left the mountains for twenty years. They have faced all the danger attributed to them by the native romancers and more, and while they found no "pound diggings" or golden bullets, they are reaping their reward at Leadville.

A few other faithful ones, however, remained, fortified themselves in Washington Gulch, living almost wholly for months at a time on game and fish, and were harassed as probably intruders deserved to be, by renegade Utes. In 1863 three men, whose names, I am sorry to say, have passed from history, still "held the fort," and with such rude sluice-boxes as they could fashion by hand, made from $0 to $20 per day. These placers have been worked almost constantly, under all sorts of discouragements, with fair results ever since. The rifle went hand in hand with the shovel, and the skeletons often exhumed in these days of peace indicate many a thrilling chapter of unwritten history.

THE PIONEER QUARTZ MINERS.

Developments in quartz mining date back to the summer of 1872, when George and Lewis Waite, two old California Gulch miners, crossed the mountains to see what could be found on the western slope. They passed over 60 miles of mineral country, failing to detect what have since developed into some of the finest gold and silver quartz districts of Gunnison, and hardly called a halt until they reached Rock Creek, an important tributary of Roaring Fork of Grand River. They were encouraged by long-since abandoned surface-diggings, and soon discovered an enormous vein of gold and silver bearing quartz, which was fitly named the "Whopper." The lode was afterwards traced across the gulch and over an adjoining mountain. A hundred miles of difficult defiles and steep heights lay between the Waites and an ore market, but they have been tunneling Whopper Mountain almost steadily ever since, quitting work only temporarily at long intervals when compelled to go back to civilization for powder and a "grub stake." Occasionally they would drive a pack mule laden with ore from the Whopper or other discoveries they made, nearly to Denver or Cañon City, and return with the necessary flour, coffee and bacon. This they continued year after year, slowly pushing to the heart of the great mountain, and patiently piling up tons upon tons of rich ore, laying up treasures for the inevitable day of reward. Although anticipating a little, I cannot resist adding here that the Waites made their well earned "home stake" in 1879, when mine hunters with capital poured into the country from Leadville.

CHIEF OURAY TO THE RESCUE.

A small band of prospectors from Denver and Golden, headed by Jim Brennon, also entered the Rock Creek district in 1872, and their reports resulted in the first organized attempt at occupying the land in 1873, when Dr. John Parsons, Professor Sylvester Richardson and thirty picked mountaineers, including an assayer, smelter, geologist and botanist, entered from Denver. Machinery for testing and reducing ore on a small scale, was taken along. This necessitated wagon transportation, and the only practicable route was via Sagauche and Los Piñnos Agency, at the southeastern boundary of the Gunnison country. The Utes had some ten years before exchanged San Luis Valley for about all of Colorado lying west of the 107th meridian, and had the whites been protected in their rights no trouble would have ensued from their going as far west as the present site of Gunnison City. The agency itself was located twenty miles east of Indian soil, but General Charles Adams, then in charge, said the expedition could only go by permission of the Utes. A heated controversy and a tie vote were finally settled by Ouray in favor of the whites. This was undoubtedly the turning point in Gunnison's history, all praise to Ouray for remnants of the expedition made valuable discoveries of gold, silver, coal, iron, copper, lead, & c., and more than this, let the outside world know of their success.

In March, 1874, a colony was formed in Denver to settle upon agricultural lands in Valley, and in the winter following twenty persons, all told, were scattered for thirty miles along Gunnison and Tomichi valleys, while the mining districts contained a still smaller showing on account of the San Juan stampede of the previous fall. The county and town of Gunnison were organized in 1876, but not until late in 1879, when prospectors fresh from Leadville and San Juan found rich gold and silver ores, and what they called carbonates at the head of Quartz Creek, near the present site of Pitkin, at the head of Tomichi River, and in other localities, did the region attract the attention it deserved. In the spring of 1879 the grand influx began. Probably twenty thousand men participated in the wonderful discoveries at Ruby Camp, Gothic, Denver, Tin Cup, Hillerton, Roaring Forks and other camps. At the height of these developments last fall came the Ute outbreak, the Thornburgh and Meeker massacres, and for weeks during the last working season at these great altitudes scarcely a day passed that did not witness some act of Indian deviltry in sight of the various mining camps, such as setting fire to the valuable forests, stealing horses or even killing a straggling prospector. Scarcely a man was to be found at many of the best camps when winter set in, and there were not adequate supplies for even the few who had the courage to remain.

WONDERFUL DEVELOPMENT OF A YEAR.

In spite of these discouragements 5,000 mines have been recorded in Gunnison County, the new discoveries at present averaging 300 per week. Several smelters and a dozen sawmills and planers are at work. The permanent population of 500 last fall has grown to 12,000, and if I may judge from appearances most of these people are here to stay. An assessed valuation of about $1,000,000 has been created here on the borders of Indian land in one year. Highways upon which daily stages run, traverse all parts of the country, and I believe the first Concord coach made its appearance in Gunnison less than sixty days ago. Seven or eight newspapers appear weekly in a field totally unoccupied three months ago. How appreciative residents are of good home literature may be judged from the fact that the first copies of three or four leading journals sold at from $50 to $100 each on the day they were issued, and I hear $50 freely offered for a complete file of eight to twelve numbers. Substantial churches, school houses and county buildings are being erected. A dozen streams are being strung for miles with houses of prosperous ranch men, thousands of cattle, sheep and horses dotting the hills, trains of rich ores are to be seen going to the railroad sixty miles away, and other trains are unloading vast quantities of mining machinery and a winter's supply of groceries.

RAILROADS FOR GUNNISON.

Two railroads, the Denver, South Park & Pacific and the Denver & Rio Grande, are coming this way, the former as fast as men and money can push it. Its management deems Gunnison's trade of sufficient importance to tunnel through Alpine Mountain 3,000 feet to get here. This great undertaking will probably delay the completion of the line to Gunnison City until midsummer, 1881, and it is a matter of current belief here that the Denver and Rio Grande people, who have a good route via Marshall Pass, will also come right along. Their recent heavy purchase of Crested Butte coal lands, the activity of their engineering parties and other factors point strongly to this conclusion. However, it takes only sixty miles of staging to reach Gunnison now, the entire distance from the Missouri River being made via the Union Pacific and Kansas Pacific railways and their connections at Denver in about fifty hours.

So much for the history of Gunnison and its accessibility. Leaving detailed description of the more important camps for future letters, I will now endeavor to convey an idea of the region's topography and most interesting natural features bearing upon its practical value as afield for both capital and labor. Gunnison county, which embraces the entire region known as the Gunnison country, lies in Western Colorado and is 110 miles long and eighty miles wide, a region nearly 10,000 square miles in extent, or of greater area than some of our Eastern States. That portion of the country, however, which the treaty now in progress will open to development, and which is of special value, is bounded on the north by Grand River and the Roaring Fork of the Grand, on the east by the Continental Divide and on the south and west mainly by the Uncompaghre River.

THE GRANDEUR OF ELK MOUNTAIN RANGE.

The Elk Mountain range, with its numerous spurs, occupies a large proportion of the area; a mountain group pronounced by our geologists one of the most remarkable in the Rockies. In this range are seven peaks rising to nearly 14,000 feet above the sea, and scores ranging from 12,000 to 13,000. Gorges and amphitheaters meet the eye on every side. Castle Peak, 14,115 feet high, rears its turrets and spires of solid granite vertically thousands of feet above the line of perpetual snow, and Snow Mass Mountain, 13,961 feet high, exhibits acres upon acres of perpetual snow and ice. The noted Teocali Mountain, named after the highest tower of the Montezumas, is also here. Scientists tell us that the vast thickness of sedimentary strata once rested upon a floor of igneous granite in a pasty or semi-pasty condition, and that these high peaks were thrust up through the overlying beds, in many instances completely overturning them for miles. Miles of granite shafts, stupendous in proportion, were shot towards heaven or horizontally. The lower ranges are covered with the finest white pine and spruce I have ever seen, while the splintered summits of a hundred peaks are vivid with their mineral stains, varying from a perfect crimson through the shades of pink to the brightest yellow, brown, and even black, with the cold glittering gray of the porphyry always ascendant. The combinations of color and effects produced on rugged mountain sides by constant seepage of water from deposits of iron, copper, and other minerals, is marvelous, while the ever-present masses of snow above and in surrounding gorges, and the dense groundwork of blue and purple of forests below add to produce landscapes so respendently beautiful and overpoweringly grand that if the artist's fancies ever does the whole justice it will be scoffed at in the Eastern

World. Think of a vast mountain of rubies crowned with acres of burnished silver and you have Ruby Peak as it appears under the bright sunlight here near Irwin every day in summer.

VAST CROPPINGS OF MINERAL.

In a region of such decided and terrific upheaval the mineral veins are naturally well defined, in many cases standing out from mountain sides in immense dykes, easily traceable on the surface for miles. It is emphatically the country of fissure veins, and yet presents the rare example of immense coal and iron beds lying in sight of the best gold and silver lodes.

The country is abundantly watered by streams fresh from the snow-fields. The principal streams all draining into Colorado River and thence to the Gulf of California are the Uncompaghre, Cochetopa, Tomichi, Taylor, East, Ohio, Eagle, Rock, Roaring Fork and Slate rivers, all noble streams, clear as crystal and full of trout, and each fed by dozens of mountain brooks and creeks. The valleys are not extensive and agriculture will never play an important part in this region's prosperity. About twenty-five miles is the greatest length of arable area in any valley, and two to three miles the greatest breadth. The elevation above the sea of habitable valleys is from 5,500 to 9,000 feet. Irrigation must be practiced everywhere to insure the growth of crops. Nestled as the valleys are among the most stupendous mountains our land affords, and richly carpeted with grasses and flowers, they present some of the most exquisitely beautiful pictures the eye will ever behold. All the bench lands, parks and lower mountain ranges are covered with bunch grass, blue-grass and other varieties of nutritious herbs, which in all cases afford excellent pasturage six months in the year, and at altitudes not exceeding 8,500 feet sustains cattle, sheep and horses winter and summer. There are probably 1,000,000 acres of all-the-year pasturage in Gunnison county.

TOPOGRAPHY OF THE MINING BELT.

It is the popular thing here, and probably the one most apropos, to liken the topography of the mining belt to a fan. At the end of the handle, in a level commanding park formed by the union of Gunnison and Tomichi rivers, and at an elevation of 7,500 feet, is the town of Gunnison. Thirty miles northward, at the top and center of the fan, are the galena and coal mines of Crested Butte, where a thirty-ton smelter has been built. From Crested Butte, as an apex, the mountains and gulches that bear the precious metals radiate as the folds of a fan. Eastward ten miles along Copper Creek are the famous ruby and native silver mines of Gothic, where quantities of ore yielding $1,000 to $3,000 silver per ton are being produced, and where the "Sylvanite" mine has accumulated in the past few weeks one car-load of ore for shipment to Newark, N. J., that will average $3,500 per ton in value. A few miles north of Gothic are Whopper, Treasure and Maroon mountains, all rich in heavy galena, and the districts in which the Waites and others have made their fortunes. East from the region just named five to fifteen miles are the East River, Cement Creek and Spring Creek gold and silver mines, the localities first named abounding in prodigious veins of silver ore worth $75 to $200 per ton, and some promising gold "finds," and the latter just now revelling in the luxury of a first-class carbonate stampede. To the southeast from ten to twenty miles further are the Hillerton, Tincup and Pitkin districts, all showing strong veins of either gold or silver in most favorable formation for permanency. The "Gold Cup" Mine, near Hillerton, has already shipped many tons of exceptionally high-grade ore, and the "Silver Islet" and "Fairview," at Pitkin, produce silver ore yielding 4,700 ounces and upward per ton. These groups complete our imaginary fan almost due east of Gunnison, twenty-five to thirty miles.

    Westward from the Crested Butte axis, eight miles, are Ruby Camp, Silver Basin and other districts, comprising what now promise to be the most important producers of extremely high grade silver ores in the Rockies. The "Forest Queen" Mine at Irwin, Ruby Camp, showing a crevice of over 100 feet and a pay streak of 4 to 8 feet yielding large masses of ruby, native and wire silver worth all the way from $500 to $10,000 per ton, and which has thus far paid $200 per foot over all expenses for every foot of shaft sunk, is only a sample among such giant veins as the "Old Shiek," "Bullion King," "Ruby King," and many others now producing high grade shipping ore. West and southwest of Irwin from three to ten miles, and completing the fan, are the great anthracite and bituminous coal deposits of Anthracite and Ohio creeks, the former coking fairly and the latter by numerous tests proving equal to the Pennsylvania anthracite the first discovery of real anthracite I have yet found west of Pennsylvania. All these districts are easily accessible by good roads from the town of Gunnison.

GUNNISON CITY THREE MONTHS OF MARVELOUS GROWTH.

With a few words about the embryo metropolis, Gunnison City, I will close for my extended tour of "the camps." A strong force of Uncompaghre Utes camped last summer on the site of Gunnison, their tepees now being replaced by some 300 houses, with a population of 1,200 or more. A number of these structures are now occupied with stocks of goods worth $40,000 to $85,000 each, from which sales are made to the extent of $10,000 to $30,000 per month each. The Bank of Gunnison is a striking example of the rapid creation of solid commercial institutions in a wilderness, its directory representing $10,000,000 of capital, and composing such men as Governor Tabor, Colorado's bonanza king. A $15,000 court house, $20,000 hotel and $7,000 public schoolhouse, besides several churches and excellent business blocks in course of erection, are a few of the surprises in this three-months-old town; but the strangest of all are real estate values. The lot occupied by the Bank of Gunnison, which cost $10 last fall, is now worth $1,500. Across the street from the bank is a log cabin that cost about $100, and its occupants pay their $40 monthly rental cheerfully. Jack Haverly, our eccentric theatrical manager, bought something like a thousand lots and a neighboring ranch in May for $30,000, and could probably double his money by their sale now. Late last fall, the Gunnison post office was the unimportant occupant of a dry-goods box. It now handles some 3,000 letters daily, and receives regularly 200 different publications.

ELK MOUNTAIN MINES.

SECOND LETTER RICHES OF THE GREAT RUBY BELT THE FOREST QUEEN, OLD SHIEK, BULLION KING, AND OTHER BONANZAS AT IRWIN ANTHRACITE COAL FIELDS, ETC.

IRWIN, RUBY CAMP, COLORADO, Aug. 28th, 1880.

"Ruby Camp," thirty miles north of Gunnison City, is without doubt the most important mineral district yet discovered in the Elk Mountain country. Ruby Belt proper, named for the large proportion of ruby silver in its ores, is six miles in length north and south and three miles in width. The great anthracite coal fields and Ruby Peak form a distinct boundary on the west, and Elk Basin, Galena District, draws a line equally distinct on the east. The entire belt of eighteen square miles lies at an altitude exceeding 10,000 feet, some rich discoveries having been made far above timber line, 12,000 and even 13,000 feet above the sea. The mineral croppings throughout the belt are the most regular, positive and stupendous I have ever seen, several of the largest veins being traceable upon the surface for a mile or more as plainly as the wall of China, and their various spurs seaming the mountain sides protrude on every hand. The veins nearly all dip twelve to fifteen degrees from the perpendicular, and in numerous instances the "hanging wall" has the appearance of a mineral bearing slate, while the lower or "foot wall" is a sort of trachyte. The pay matter in most instances has started at the surface in the shape of the greenish chlorides of silver, milling from 500 to 1,000 ounces of silver to the ton. At a depth of three to six feet ruby silver (50 to 60 per cent pure silver) brittle silver and native silver, have manifested themselves, notably in the Forest Queen, Ruby King and Ruby Chief lodes, and at greater depths sulphurets of silver. To a depth of 40 or 50 feet the ore is of almost unexampled richness and has not often proved so refractory as to necessitate any very complicated process in treatment, but arsenical iron and zinc are coming in quite strongly in some of the deeper shafts. While these are the miner's most uncomfortable apparition and zinc is so hated that he calls it "black jack"— they nevertheless auger well for the strength and permanency of veins. There is but little lead in the Ruby mines. Over 1,000 claims have been recorded, and you may imagine Ruby Belt is pretty well "staked."

THE FIRST DISCOVERY.

The first discovery was the Ruby Chief, located June 5, 1879, by Messrs, Brennand & Diffebaugh. It was easily found by the enormous croppings, and the first ton of crevice matter blasted down yielded $300. The crevice is 14 feet wide. Two tunnels 200 feet apart, cutting the vein at right angles some 50 feet below the surface, disclose an ore body from one to two feet thick whose product is 837 ounces silver per ton for first-class rock, 416 ounces for second- class, and 200 ounces for third-class. An 18-inch vein of 2,000-ounce ore has been found in another opening. About 600 feet above the Ruby Chief, and along the south base of Ruby Peak, is the Old Shiek lode, the second discovery in the camp, having been located only a few hours after the first, and on which there are four locations of 1,500 feet each. The width of the lode on the surface and so far as developments have disclosed is from 60 to 75 feet, and the pay vein 15 to 20 feet. Specimens of ruby and brittle silver, assaying from $1,000 to $10,000 per ton, can be found upon the cropping on almost every rod of this mammoth vein. It is claimed that ore and rock together, just as it is blasted from the entire width of 15 to 20 feet, will yield an average of 100 ounces silver per ton. Developments so far as they have progressed look like the quarrying of stone from an immense stone-quarry. The Howard Extension, Old Mexico and Chloride Deposit are the other important locations on the Shiek lode. Numerous shafts, cuts and tunnels exposing the great vein at depths ranging from 25 to 100 feet show substantially the same ore-body as above described. Three assays made from a large dump of Howard Extension ore, to determine the values of all the matter being taken from the 20-foot vein, resulted as follows: $334, $166 and $840 silver to the ton. Proceeding across a gulch to a neighboring mountain, one and one half miles east of the Old Shiek, is the Justice, owned by Messrs. Thompson Brothers, of Ruby, and Field and Farwell, the merchant princes of Chicago. It is on a direct line with Old Shiek, and is believed to be the extension of that lode on account of its similar prodigious size and the character and dip of its vein. It protrudes from the surface a dozen feet or more. Some 25 tons of top rock ready for shipment will, from careful sampling, yield 500 to 600 ounces silver per ton. Dozens of spurs or offshoots from these veins are being developed, nearly all having more or less rich shipping ore out ready for the advent of smelters.

JACK HAVERLY'S GREAT PURCHASES.

Half a mile south of the Old Shiek lies the Bullion King and Monte Christo, discovered in July, 1879, by Ule Bros. & McCloud, and sold to J. H. Haverly & Co. in December when there was no semblance of development, but an open cut twelve feet deep on the former for $105,000. This region is probably the only one in all Christendom where ten and twelve-foot holes sell frequently for from $100,000 to $200,000, and Jack Haverly is one of the kind of men who are captured by "big croppings." These claims are on one vein and a 50-foot shaft exposed an 18-inch pay streak. Enough ore yielding 400 to 1,200 ounces of silver per ton to pay the expense of the development noted, as well as other open cuts, &c., has been shipped. During my visit, a blast in the Monte Christo knocked down a line lot of ore fairly mottled with ruby silver. First-class hoisting works will be erected on the Bullion King this fall. Mr. Haverly, who has Mr. E. A. Buck, of the New York *Spirit of the Times*, and Mr. C. S. Boucher, a Pennsylvania journalist, interested with him, is dabbling in about every conceivable enterprise that promises a "good thing" in Gunnison, San Juan and other new mineral districts. He owns a controlling interest in 2,000 lots in Gunnison, Irwin and Crested Butte, large tracts of coal lands in Washington Gulch, a dozen silver veins at Ruby and Gothic, a three-fourths interest in the *Gunnison News*, several ranches near Gunnison, and two stores In the same place, a sawmill, mines by the dozen in San Juan and Silver Cliff, and keeps eight prospecting companies in the field to find more. It is a serious question down in this country what is to be done to appease such an appetite.

THE FOREST QUEEN— ONE HUNDRED THOUSAND DOLLARS FOR AN HOUR'S WORK.

But the most famous mine of all Gunnison is the Forest Queen, and you cannot tarry in Irwin an hour without being asked, "Have you seen the Forest Queen?" Well, it is enough of a mine to alone support such a town as Irwin when properly developed, and its history is worth repeating. A "tenderfoot," named W. A. Fisher, who had driven all the way from Maryland with an ox team, and who had never seen a mine, arrived at the lower end of Ruby Gulch on the evening of July 7, 1879. The grade was very steep and the mud almost bottomless at his point of entry, and his wagon became almost hopelessly mired. A spectator, O. P. Mace, succeeded in pulling him out with a strong pair of mules, and Fisher gratefully told him he would give him a half interest in the first mine he found. Mace little thought the kindness, small as it was, would net him $100,000; but the next morning Fisher started up the nearest gulch, which happened to be that leading to the head of Coal Creek. Not more that 200 yards above the town he found a tremendous dyke or vein of quartz crossing the gulch and laid plainly bare by the constant action of the stream. Verdant as he was he could not help seeing ruby, native and brittle silver. The claim on the north side of the creek he named the Forest Queen, and that on the south side the Ruby King. He gave Mace his choice, which settled on the Ruby King, and then was left with that portion of the lode which has created such a furor in the mining world. Strangely enough, Mace sold his portion, with less than ten feet of the rock removed, for $100,000, while Fisher, who made about the same developments on what has generally been conceded the better mine, sold for $40,000.

The Forest Queen vein is from 100 to 125 feet wide, its course northeast and southwest, and its "dip" from the vertical 12 degrees to the east. It protrudes from the surface in mammoth ledges of hard, flinty quartz for nearly 1,000 feet. The pay-streak, running from 4 to 8 feet in width, is composed of just such material as referred to in notes concerning the Old Shiek and other Ruby mines, with this difference, that throughout the 1000 feet of croppings, ore worth anywhere from

FIVE THOUSAND TO FIFTEEN THOUSAND DOLLARS PER TON

is found in respectable quantities. Near the deepest shaft the vein has been cut down some 20 feet and graded to make room for extensive hoisting works, a surface some 100 feet square being thus exposed. Not only is the main pay-streak here plainly discernable, but a dozen smaller streaks of ruby, brittle silver, native silver and chlorides, assaying high up in the thousands, and diffused throughout the 100 feet of vein matter. Last fall $60,000 worth of ore was taken out of a cut some 60 feet long and 10 feet deep. Over $40,000 worth of ore was taken out during the summer at a total expense for mining of $700. This ran up to $1000 per ton. A shaft 4x12 feet is down 70 feet, having passed through solid shipping ore all the way, and a tunnel is now in 100 feet from point of discovery at the creek bed, also disclosing immense bodies of high-grade mineral. The ore taken from the shaft alone, which is always considered "dead work," has paid for all developments, for the employment of thirty men, for timbering, grading and expensive hoisting works, and $200 per foot net profit besides. The ore has not been assorted, but shipped to Denver and other points just as it came from the vein. I have before me statements from Senator Hill's smelting works at Denver showing that ore averaged 619 ounces of silver to the ton in car load lots, and another shipment taken from within four feet of the surface that returned $783 per ton, a small percentage being gold. The ore can undoubtedly be assorted so as to run anywhere from $5,000 to $10,000, for I saw at the mines a dozen sacks, part of one or two tons of specimens selected each month, and these lots have averaged 6,000 ounces of silver per ton. I descended into the shaft just after two blasts were fired, and found nearly two tons of rich ore strewn over the bottom, fragments of ruby silver as richly colored as the name would indicate, and masses weighing two hundred to three hundred pounds, full of brittle, native and ruby silver.

The Forest Queen is indeed a "royal find," with its capital of $1,000,000 easily in sight. There are 10,000 shares of stock of a par value of $100, and the confidence of some holders in the future of the property can be judged from the fact that there is a standing offer out for 2,000 shares at par. The principal owners are Colonel D. C. Dodge, General Manager of the Denver and Rio Grande Railway; George M. Pullman, of Pullman-car fame; Mr. Woerishoffer, the New York banker; R. W. Woodbury, proprietor of the *Denver Daily Times*, and General Palmer. President of the Denver and Rio Grande Railway. Colonel W. T. Holt, a prominent manufacturer of Portland, Me., is President of the company, and L. R. Thompson, the organizer of the company, is Superintendent. No effort has been made to ship ore, as the mine is being systematically developed with an eye to a future permanent output. About two hundred tons have gone to market this season, and the average output after next week will be about twenty tors per day. Good judges say that the product can be run up to $10,000 per day at a week's notice.

The Ruby King is a second edition of the Forest Queen, the vein being only broken, as already noted, by Coal Creek, and the cleft being less than six feet. The main pay-streak is now 3 feet 10 inches of solid mineral that will average 500 ounces of silver to the ton. A 65-foot shaft and 70-foot drift have found the ore body without a break, and at one point a drift of 22 feet 6 inches across the vein disclosed pay ore all the way. Ore will not be raised for six months, except that which lies in the way of development. This dead work alone produces six tons of rich ore daily. Col. W. T. Holt is the owner of this prize, and with his 10,000 head of cattle and 15,000 sheep roaming the Colorado plains, as well as his heavy manufacturing interests, he can well afford to carry out an extensive system of development explained to me, rather than to strip the mine for present profit.

A RANCHMAN'S RISE FROM WANT TO AFFLUENCE.

A mile northwest of Irwin, overlooking beautiful Lake Brennand, are the Lead Chief and Little Chief. The veins run parallel east and west and are close enough together to be embraced in the 300 feet allowed one location. The Lead Chief was discovered July 1, 1879, by A. T. Gilkerson, under circumstances more interesting than attended the finding of the Forest Queen. Gilkerson had tried his luck in the mines of various Western States and Territories for twelve years with very poor success and was really in destitute circumstances. He had loaded his effects in a wagon at Gothic, some twenty miles from here, and was about to do the same with his almost naked family and start on his wearisome journey across the plains to his old home in the far East. Going to the pasture for his mules, he found one of them dead. He had no credit, could not buy another animal or get work, and leaving his family with the few provisions they had, he walked hither in hopes of receiving at least temporary employment. Pausing near the present site of the Lead Chief buildings to rest and eat a scanty lunch with a companion, R. A. Duncan, he took occasion to follow the trail a few yards down to Anthracite Creek for a drink, and on the way noticed an inviting ledge that had been laid bare by horses' hoofs. It was "prospected," the Lead Chief discovered, and soon its marvelously rich specimens of native ruby and wire silver attracted the attention of capitalists, and last March he was made

FIFTY THOUSAND DOLLARS RICHER BY ITS SALE,

Duncan pocketing a like amount. The family was soon brought over from Crested Butte, loaded on sleds, and eight mountaineers on snow shoes pulled them for two days over eight to twenty feet of snow to Ohio Valley, where more comfortable conveyances could be used to carry them out to civilization. Gilkerson has purchased a splendid farm in Cache La Poudre Valley, this State, and will live comfortably hereafter. I should not forget, however, that his boys, Charlie and Willie, aged seven and nine respectively, discovered the Little Chief while their father was busy in his work of development on the Lead Chief. They dug faithfully for weeks in the vicinity for "blind lodes," were finally successful, and their claim (which has been sold at a handsome figure to the Lead Chief Company) is now believed to be the "mother lode," as it shows much the stronger vein. These veins are from four to six feet wide, with pay streaks averaging about one foot. Shafts are down forty-five to seventy feet, disclosing zinc blende and iron pyrites literally flaked with native and wire silver. Several lots of ore have been shipped, yielding splendidly. Colonel E. P. Jacobson, a prominent Denver attorney, and others own these claims. Hoisting works will be put up for the Little Chief this fall.

HUNDREDS OF PROMISING PROSPECTS.

In sight of Irwin are hundreds of promising "prospects," many of which are accumulating ores, similar to those already described, for shipment, and probably a hundred of which have changed hands at figures ranging from $5,000 to $25,000 each. Then there are groups of worthy properties clustered all over the surrounding mountains from one to three miles away. Among the more important of the latter are the Grant Park Mines, one mile to the east. The Fairview, Ella, Eureka and Diablo are the best developed lodes here, and a striking peculiarity is their all lying parallel and just about 325 feet apart. They all carry a hard, white quartz, running high in ruby and native silver, and are therefore absolutely free from refractory metals. The crevices are 4 to 6 feet wide, with pay veins 8 inches to 3 feet thick, and mill runs of the ore show a value of 200 to 1,000 ounces silver per ton. The Eureka, only 15 feet deep, sold a day or two ago for $18,000, and the Thompson Bros., of Forest Queen notoriety, bought the Fairview last spring, with only a 10 foot prospect hole, for $10,000. They have since refused $30,000 after sinking it 15 feet deeper. The Fairview is shipping $300 ore.

Four miles northwest of Irwin, beyond Ruby Peak, is Silver Basin, where a company of Texas capitalists and others are operating on the General Sales lode, a monster deposit protruding from the surface from five to twenty feet for four miles. Mill runs at Leadville of ore from some of these claims returned $527 silver per ton. The Alabama and Poland also show immense croppings of silver-bearing galena. Some fifty claims are being worked in Silver Basin.

SENATOR ELAINE'S INVESTMENT.

One and one-half miles north of Irwin, in Susquehanna Basin, is the Independence Mine, the property of Senator Blaine and Lieutenant-Governor Tabor. The present owners were glad to get an "entering wedge" of a one-half interest last winter at $65,000, and have since paid a good round sum for the entire mine. The vein is of gigantic proportions, and is readily traced on the surface for a mile. There are three feet of heavy galena ore, running well in silver, at the bottom of a forty-foot shaft. Near by, in Elk Basin, Messrs. Fields & Co. are working the Elk, Brittle Silver, King and several other claims out of a total of thirty-five owned by them there. Eighteen-inch pay streaks, showing richly in gray copper, native and ruby silver ore, are the interesting features of half a dozen of these prospects.

VAST DEPOSITS OF ANTHRACITE COAL.

Hardly second in importance to the silver veins of Ruby Camp are the deposits of anthracite coal. It may be noted here that the presence in vast quantities of coal contiguous to the precious metals, and the indications of slate in the wall-rock of some of the very best silver veins, has proved quite a bug-bear in the eyes of capitalists. Indeed, "experts" from Leadville and elsewhere, have maintained that when the silver veins are worked to a great depth the entire Ruby Belt will be found underlaid with coal. Other well-informed mining engineers and geologists claim that there is a well-defined break or "fault" of some thousands of feet between the coal belt and the silver belt, and that from the very nature of their position it is certain the two can never mingle. I have been over all the ground carefully, and it would seem to me, from the rapid "dip" of the coal in the direction of the silver belt, that the veins of the former thus far uncovered will never be reached by shafts of silver mines until some invention will enable the modern miner to sink far deeper than the well-known "dead line" of heat encountered in the oldest European mines. Granting that coal may supplant silver here at some time in the distant future, the enthusiastic Ruby mine owner insists that he has enough ore in sight to revolutionize the silver market, and "don't care a continental what happens after that."

The anthracite coal measures lie three miles southwest of Irwin, on a branch of Anthracite Creek. They were easily discovered, about a year ago, through the masses of "float" found far down the creek by Messrs. Brown, Thompson & Co., of Irwin, who have secured about 1,000 acres of land in the vicinity of the croppings. The Denver, South Park & Pacific Railway Company has also come into possession of 1,000 acres adjoining on the north. The creek cuts through a narrow gorge about 125 feet deep, exposing the deposit on both sides for nearly three fourths of a mile. The first vein near the surface, commonly called a horizontal one, but pitching rapidly to the north, is from four to six feet thick. Between this and the bed of the creek are two other veins of less magnitude, while the creek bed for a mile or more is full of coal and slate debris. Thousands of tons of excellent anthracite are exposed, which can be mined at a trifling expense not over 50 cents per ton. One tunnel in fifty feet and several others not so far demonstrate that the top vein grows thicker as progress is made. The deposit is overlaid by a ledge of sandstone, which makes a roof almost as perfect as a plastered ceiling. The same vein is found cropping out of a mountain half a mile east of the creek. A geologist who has made an examination of the deposit states that the different veins exposed in the creek banks probably consolidate a short distance under ground and form one immense bed 50 to 100 feet thick. Following is an analysis of the coal as made at the United States Assay Office, Denver: Fixed carbon, 93; water and volatile matter, 2; ash, 5; total, 100. Compared with Pennsylvania anthracite, this coal carries the palm. It is not quite so heavy, but the average of several analyses of the best Pennsylvania coal, as stated by Professor Hayden, shows a smaller percentage of fixed carbon than the Gunnison article. Following is the average of the Pennsylvania coal: Fixed carbon, 88.046; ash, 7.661; water and volatile matter, 5.811. The Denver, South Park & Pacific Railroad survey lies within easy reach of the Gunnison anthracite, and the road will probably be completed that far inside of eighteen months. Besides supplying a heavy demand throughout the Rocky Mountains, it is not extravagant to anticipate coal from this deposit soon going to the prairie States of the Missouri Valley, which are now heavy consumers of Pennsylvania coal. Our trans-Missouri railways could at any other season than cattle-moving times well afford to haul coal from this region to Kansas and Nebraska and even Western Missouri and Iowa points at the rate charged from, say, Reading or Pottsville, considering that they pull at least half their cars eastward empty. Since writing my last letter I have learned that there is another deposit of anthracite coal along Rock Creek, about twenty-five miles north of Irwin, those two being the only ones yet discovered in all the vast country lying between Pennsylvania and the Pacific Ocean.

EVERY NEWCOMER A PROSPECTOR.

Ruby Camp, like all others remote from smelting works and having high freight rates to pay on all ores shipped, should hardly be judged in the light of its past or even present production. Its history, a series of discouragements thus far, needs only to be briefly touched to show that the richest mining districts in the world may struggle along a year without attracting special attention. As already noted, the first discoveries were made but little more than one year ago. The first ore uncovered was so fabulously rich that every miner or newcomer became a prospector. He would not work for others in a region that offered such a seductive showing for him soon to become an employer. It was then clearly impossible for any mine-owner to develop his "prospect," no matter what wages he would offer for the muscle. Lumber for timbering shafts or asking other necessary improvements was not obtainable last season at any price; it was selling at $200 per 1,000 feet as late as sixty days ago. There was no market for ores last season, and no way to take them to the railroad, even if they were worth $1 per pound. At present ores must pay a tribute of from $35 to $45 per ton freightage to Pueblo and Denver, and the expense of smelting is from $25 to $40 per ton. Adding these sums and you have a larger figure than the ores of any mining camp in Colorado will yield on an average.

TIMES THAT TRIED MEN'S SOULS.

To totally stop development, just as the assessment work (ten feet of sinking) was done on the last claims last fall, the Indian troubles commenced. The woods were full of savages who set fire to the timber, stole stock, picked off straggling miners, and sent in word that the Thornburgh and Meeker massacres were only the beginning if the pioneers insisted in holding the country. In a few weeks scarcely a soul was left of the thousands who had roamed the hills.

When hostilities ceased the snows began to fall, and no supplies could have been brought into the country even if miners had been willing to make the long tramp back here from the Colorado settlement in the face of a six months' winter. The faithful few who remained lived principally on "game straight." Supplies were not brought in until last May, when it cost $150 to $200 per ton to freight them from the railroad about one hundred miles away. These were carried on the backs of the indomitable miners for the last dozen miles. The snow laid in Irwin from ten to fifteen feet deep up to May, and the best mining country was deluged with mud and water until about July 1. It will thus be seen that there has really been no mining done here previous to six weeks ago. The old games of "freeze-out," in which prosperous owners of interests in mines always take more or less time to crowd out poor partners, are played in Ruby Camp as elsewhere. Many good properties will on this account lie idle at least all this season.

A WORD TO CAPITALISTS.

Again, the prospectors here generally have rather an exalted idea of the value of their claims, because so many ten-foot holes like the Forest Queen, Lead Chief, Bullion King, &c., have sold for from $50,000 to $150,000 each. They are holding for like prices, and spoil many a sale that could be effected for from $5,000 to $20,000. A word to capitalists may not be amiss here. There is not a better region in the Rocky Mountains in which to pick up claims that promise to develop into good paying properties at a depth of from 50 to 200 feet than right here in Ruby Camp. But don't come now to buy. About November 1, when the average prospector has an almost unconquerable penchant for getting to milder climes, and when his stock of flour and bacon has run so low that a long winter of want stares him in the face, and when he thoroughly realizes that for at least six months the deep snows will prevent his looking for more mines and also prevent the capitalist from coming in to buy those he already owns, you can strike him at "bedrock." Then a few hundreds will accomplish what thousands would barely accomplish now. I have in mind a sale that was consummated for $50,000 last November in a neighboring district, and the mine was held firmly at $400,000 during the preceding three months. The purchaser made $40,000 by delaying the purchase the last three weeks, and the original holders were constantly improving the property at that. This line of action will apply equally well to speculations in town lots or other property, and if a loan is effected in the fall hereabouts, the borrower is fortunate if he gets it on good security at anything short of four percent per month.

THE REDUCTION OF ORES.

No ores are yet smelted in all this Gunnison country, although several smelters are completed and under way. The Goodenough Milling and Mining Company is erecting a 30-ton smelter here, embodying the best principles of the dry-crushing process. Two Brackner furnaces, one Blake crusher, six Morey & Sperry amalgamating pans and ten 750-pound stamps are the leading features to start with, and the buildings and 125 horse-power engine will admit of doubling the capacity. The cost will be $75,000. Samples of ores from several of the twenty mines owned by the company were submitted to the Balbachs, at Newark, N. J., and to eminent authority at New York, the various tests resulting in the selection of this machinery. An abundance of timber, building rock, sand and water are found within a few rods of these works. A Georgetown (Col.) smelting firm has about concluded arrangements for the immediate erection here of extensive works. Of the smelting works at Crested Butte and Scofield, I shall write particularly hereafter, but I may say here in a general way that vast bodies of the finest pine and spruce timber I have seen in the Rockies are here; that there is an abundance of coking and anthracite coal, lime and different forms of iron ore for fluxing, splendid water power everywhere, and a good variety of ores in various camps for smelting; in fact that nothing seems wanting in the way of natural facilities to constitute this a perfect field for the reduction of ores on an extensive scale.

LIVING EXPENSES, WAGES, RENTS, ETC.

Expenses of living at Irwin may be taken as an average throughout the Gunnison country, prices at the town of Gunnison being somewhat lower and at more distant camps higher. Board and lodging is quoted $12 to $15 per week; day board, $7 to $9; single meals or lodging, 50 to 75 cents; "batch-ing," where parties do their own cooking in their own cabins, costs $4 to $6 per week; an Irwin "hair-cut" costs 75 cents; baths, $1. Cottages or cabins of three rooms each are in demand at $15 to $25 per month; best steaks, 25 cents per pound; bacon, 19 cents; potatoes, 10 cents; onions and cabbage, 12 1-2 cents; butter, 45 to 60 cents; oats, 8 cents; corn, 8 cents per pound, and hay, $160 per ton. Rents of stores, $50 to $175 per month; of lots 22-feet front, $25 per month. Hotels and lodging houses are thus far either mere shells or tents. Miners and good mechanics of every class are in demand, wages running about as follows: Miners, underground, $4 per day; on surface, $3.50; blacksmiths and machinists, $4; carpenters, $3.50; bricklayers, masons and plasterers, $5; laborers, teamsters, &c., $2.50.

INDUSTRY REWARDED.

Irwin boasts about 300 buildings and 75 business firms, who seem to drive a good trade. About 3,500 men get mail at the Irwin post office. The latter is alike a curiosity and credit to its present governing official, Mr. "W. L. G. Soule." This gentleman was one of the few who held the fort all last winter, and his office was for months at a time ten to fifteen feet under the snow. Business was of course dull, and Mr. Soule, anticipating the rush of this summer, whittled out 168 "boxes" for regular patrons and a large case of pigeon-holes for the "general delivery" with his pocket knife. The department has never furnished him a pair of scales, so he improvised them with two tin plates for platters, wire from a broom-handle connecting them with the wooden beam, which balances nicely on a section of an old knife blade. He also made his own weights out of scraps of metal. The office is often out of stamps for weeks at a time, and is a boss borrower, although it deserves to rank as second class. Soule pined for other worlds to conquer after rigging up the paraphernalia described above, and finally went to whittling out snow-shoes at $3 per pair. He succeeded in buying several lots near his office from the proceeds at $10 a piece, and he is now selling them at from $800 to $1,500 each. During the winter he lived on flour and water, the former being carried thirty miles on the backs of miners and selling at $30 to $40 per 100 pounds.

CRESTED BUTTE.

THIRD LETTER THE FUTURE SMELTING CENTRE OF THE GUNNISON COUNTRY, SILVER, LEAD, IRON AND COKING COAL.

CRESTED BUTTE, COLORADO, September 1, 1880.
Journeying eastward down Coal Creek Valley, eight miles from Ruby Camp, we find Crested Butte, the point generally accepted as the future smelting centre of the Gunnison country. The village of some 300 souls is romantically located at the junction of Coal Creek, Slate River and Washington Gulch. High mountains, covered with a heavy growth of pine and spruce, rise abruptly above it on the west, and a beautiful meadow stretches off a mile to the east, where the sharp pinnacled mountain which gives the town its name makes its almost vertical rise of nearly 4,000 feet. The altitude of the town is about 8,500 feet. An important mineral belt on the east, west, and north slopes gradually towards the valley of Slate River and Crested Butte as a common centre. Peeler Basin, Oh Be Joyful Gulch, Slate River Basin, Poverty Gulch, Washington Gulch, Red Well Basin, Coal Creek Basin, and other producers of heavy galena ores are all reached from Crested Butte by water grade at distances varying from two to five miles. The ore from the surrounding mines (except from Peeler Basin) although not so high grade as much of the Ruby district ore, is far less refractory, and lying in usually large bodies, will be cheaply mined. It also carries a very large percentage of lead which adapts it admirably for treatment in connection with the dry ores of adjoining camps. The Coal Creek mines on the east, which line the road almost all the way to Ruby Camp, eight miles away, show heavy galena ores two to six feet wide running from 40 to 70 per cent lead and 30 to 100 ounces of silver per ton. North of Coal

Creek two or three miles is Oh Be Joyful Gulch, with its tributaries Peeler and Red Well basins. The Peeler Basin veins thus far attract the more attention because they are developing ore almost identical in character and richness with those of Ruby Camp. They show fine

MASSES OF RUBY AND NATIVE SILVER,

as well as the refractory elements, arsenical iron, zinc and antimony. Red Well Basin abounds in tremendous fissure veins of low-grade lead ores which are steadily improving in richness as depth is attained. The Colorado State is a promising claim, showing at the breast of a 50-foot tunnel six feet of ore, which assays from 10 to 50 ounces. A $10,000 sale of a group of Red Well mines has just been effected and the owner will push developments rapidly the coming winter. Poverty Gulch, north of the basins just named, rebuts its name, considering that it is now sending out ore from the Yankee Blade and other claims which carries 500 and 600 ounces of silver. Streaks of gray copper in these veins assay up to $1,400 per ton, and carry the general average to a neat figure. Slate River Basin and tributaries, lying north of Crested Butte ten miles, boast of some very good "prospects," the Iowa, Daisy and Forsaken, I believe, having changed hands at good figures. The former is shown by an open cut to be some thirty feet wide. Three veins of galena ore, eight inches to three feet wide, running 100 ounces in silver, and other smaller seams of equal richness, are found diffused throughout the crevices.

WASHINGTON GULCH MINES.

Washington Gulch, six miles north of Crested Butte, in which gulch mining operations have been carried on with good results for twenty years, is rapidly turning into a first-class quartz camp. But one placer claim is being worked, result $5 to $10 per day to the man while the hills surrounding are resounding with echoes of pick and blast. The Elk Mountain Gold and Silver Mining Company, composed largely of Atchison, Topeka and Santa Fe Railroad men owns eleven promising claims. The best showing thus far is made upon the Highland and Gypsy, both being down nearly 100 feet and showing well-defined true fissure veins. Native gold, silver, ruby silver and black sulphurets of silver are found in small veins. Four lots of ore, claimed by the company to be average grades from four different mines, ran as follows at the Philadelphia Mint: Gypsy lode, 250 ounces of silver per ton; Highland, 550; Gavitt, 650; and Miner's Delight, 400 ounces silver per ton. The Baxter lode shows wonderful assays, 400 ounces silver and $450 in gold being the result of one of them. A 300-foot tunnel on the Miner's Delight is about to place that property in excellent trim for a good yield. About every camp in the Gunnison country claims to have found carbonates, and Washington Gulch is no exception. But the showing is thus far so small here that it is hardly worth noting. A capitalist named Hayden is preparing to open some of the extensive bars of the gulch with hydraulics, and his large outlay to lead the necessary water supply where it is wanted will enable him to break ground in good earnest next season.

In my perambulations here I find numerous large veins of galena ores whose croppings will yield 50 to 70 ounces silver per ton, and 30 to 75 per cent lead. These would be bonanzas in the northern part of Colorado, almost anywhere within 100 miles of Denver and there are at least twenty-five prospects or mines in the districts noted above that in thirty days could be placed in condition to yield 20 tons of ore each, worth on an average $90 per ton. The principal trouble is, every man is "mine-poor." The average prospector, be he tenderfoot or old-timer, would in his greed "to own the country" sooner hunt for ten mines and starve sinking a ten-foot hole (which he knows few intelligent capitalists will look at) on each of them, than to concentrate his energies in doing 100 feet of work on one good prospect with a show not only of taking good wages out of every foot of ore, but of selling his single developed property at a handsome figure.

RICH IRON ORES AND WONDERFUL MARBLE QUARRIES.

Along Coal Creek, two miles east of Crested Butte, amid some of the best silver mines, is an iron swamp covering 500 acres. The bog will average ten feet in depth and is 60 per cent iron. It is entirely free from silica or other matter that would prevent an easy conversion into what is known as second-class iron in commerce. It is at present valuable only as a flux at the Crested Butte Smelting Works. Along Slate River, eight miles north of Crested Butte, is a fine deposit of perfectly pure hematite, and in an opposite direction, about the same distance, magnetic iron of a wonderful strength is scattered over the sides of a steep mountain. Deposits of red hematite are also found in Oh Be Joyful Gulch, four miles away. A superb white limestone, also utilized by the smelter, and a pure bluish limestone in inexhaustible quantities are found four miles away. Slate River gets its name from the large deposits of excellent slate found along it. East River, six miles distant, also abounds in this article. Both deposits are of a superior quality, especially for roofing purposes, an item worthy of note in connection with the fact that the entire slate supply of the Plains and Rocky Mountains comes from far east of the Mississippi. Between the head of Slate River and Rock Creek, on the north side of the main Elk Mountain, and on a spur of the latter called Crystal Mountain, is a vast deposit of most beautiful marble. The deposit is seemingly the basin of an extinct volcano, and consists of mammoth ledges of crystallized or granular marble of almost every shade and color, and of great variety of texture, from the finest Italian to the coarsest grained, soft yellow. The purest white and most delicate shades of pink are represented, some of these taking an exquisite finish.

COAL, MOST IMPORTANT OF ALL.

These various items, important and interesting as they may be, sink into insignificance when compared to Crested Butte's vast measures of coking coal. The coal is plainly exposed on both banks of Coal Creek in the outskirts of the village, and the vein now worked, five to seven feet thick, evidently underlies several thousand acres. A tunnel is in twenty-five feet on the left bank, and one over 200 feet on the right bank of the stream. From the latter the coal is conveyed on cars to a level plat along the stream 100 yards below, and there burned in the open air in small pyramidal heaps into coke. The coal resembles Blossburg coal, and is 75 per cent coke.

Following is the analysis: Water, 1.55; volatile matter, 22.80; fixed carbon, 68.70; ash, 7; total, 100. The coke contains three-tenths of 1 per cent sulphur, and 11.04 per cent ash. Assayers and smelters who have tested the coke say it is so near equal to the best Pennsylvania article that the importation of the latter will cease when the railroad gets within twenty-five miles of Crested Butte. This coke is used throughout the Gunnison country and is sold at the mines for from $7 to $8 per ton. The coal is greatly prized for use in forges. The Iowa Mining and Smelting Company owns 320 acres; the Denver & Rio Grande Railway, 1,000 acres; and Judge Grant, of the Leadville Smelting works, 160 acres of these coal lands.

The Iowa Mining and Smelting Company, Howard F. Smith, superintendent, has invested $100,000 in coal lands, smelting works and other property at Crested Butte, and affords about the only market yet established for Gunnison ores. The smelting works are simply designed for reducing ores into base or lead bullion, using calcining and blast furnaces. The present capacity is twelve tons per day and the buildings are so constructed as to afford ample room for more than doubling the output. At present the company is engaged principally in buying and sampling ores for shipment to Colorado and Eastern smelting and refining works. As an evidence of the general good grade of ores handled here I will add that the thousands of assays made this summer from hundreds of different mines and prospects, the samples, of course, coming from all sorts of rock from the surface down, have shown an average yield of 36.4 ounces silver to the ton; omitting all that ran less than fifteen ounces the average came to

ONE HUNDRED AND FORTY OUNCES SILVER PER TON.

These assays included only the heavy galena ores of the Crested Butte country, and included none of the very rich shipments or specimens that were received from Ruby Camp.

A mile and a half north of Crested Butte, in a romantic dell along Slate River, are some cold white sulphur springs. The waters are recommended as universally efficacious, and their strength is to some extent indicated by the flakes of pure white sulphur which coat everything they come in contact with. Near by is a beautiful lake, as blue and for aught the residents know as deep as the open sea. Four miles from the village, on Cement Creek, are hot and cold soda springs which together throw off enough water to heal a multitude. These valuable properties are, I believe, as yet unclaimed, but the ambitious Coloradoan will probably soon have them fenced, covered up or dammed for the good of suffering humanity and his pocket. What with its magnificent scenery, its comparatively low altitude, these various mineral springs and its proximity to some of the best fishing in the land, as well as to the favorite haunts of bear, deer and mountain sheep, Crested Butte should upon the approach of the iron horse attract many besides mere searchers for the silver dollar. Crested Butte is about thirty miles from Gunnison City and ninety from the nearest railroad point. The indications are that one narrow-gauge line at least will be here by August, 1881.

GOTHIC AND ROCK CREEK.

FOURTH LETTER— THE SYLVANITE HOW OBADIAH SANDS, OF CHICAGO, STRUCK IT RICH WHEN BANKRUPT IN HEALTH AND PURSE A SPLENDID FIELD FOR THE PROSPECTOR.

GOTHIC CITY, COLORADO, September 5th, 1880.

Rocky Mountain mining camps are phenomenally alike in one important respect. Each swears by one great mine. There may be a thousand claims recorded in the camp, and every owner with a sharp eye to business declares his particular property is a bonanza. But simmer it all down to a question of superiority upon the part of one camp over another, and you mass its sentiment forthwith upon one great leading mine "that is the biggest thing in the world, sir." Gothic is a peculiar illustration of this. It has the "Sylvanite" mine, perched like an eagle's eyrie among towering cliffs far above "timberline," five miles away, which it stands ready to pit against any treasure vault yet uncovered in the Rockies. There is no more seductive bit of mining history than that linked with this wonderful property, a property to which the flourishing town owes its existence and as I have had long and close acquaintance with the central figure I can vouch for every word of it.

Obadiah Sands, well known all over the West, for a number of years past as the proprietor of the Sands House, Chicago, was stricken down several years ago with dangerous nervous disorders plainly the result of overwork and as a consequence relinquished his business, temporarily as he thought, to other hands, going to a noted health resort for a season. The "other hands" ruined not only his business but plunged the institution almost hopelessly into debt, and Sands returned to Chicago, unimproved in health, to find himself worse than "dead broke." Giving up his business there, he borrowed a hundred or two from a relative, and in the winter of 1879 came to Colorado on a mattress, as he now expresses it, "to die." Upon reaching' Cañon City, with a shattered constitution, with a family behind evidently destined to soon come to want, and no lack of creditors to haunt him, he grasped at the first straw that presented itself; that was

MINING BY PROXY.

John and David Jennings, old hunters and prospectors, happened to be wintering at Cañon City, and a chance acquaintance formed with them finally budded into an arrangement by which they were to start for the then almost mythical Gunnison country early in the spring, taking about all the money he had as a "grub stake," and agreeing to give him half of everything found if he would regularly contribute $80 per month towards keeping up expenses. They had not completed their first month's work when Sands was informed that they had "struck it rich," and was requested to come into the wilderness, a distance of 200 miles, to see for himself. The Colorado climate had meanwhile restored his health to such an extent, at least, that he was able to walk as much of the way as was necessary. The discovery was made May 28, 1879, and by midsummer Sands, without investing a dollar above the value of ore taken out, had concluded arrangements for the sale of a large portion of his half to David H. Sherman, of New York City; Ira D. Warren, present secretary of the company; Dr. Linderman, Mr. Dutcher, (one of Vanderbilt's right-hand men), and others, his different sales of "Sylvanite" bringing him nearly $100,000 in cash, and the profits of the mine with his present small holding of stock adding a good many thousands as his net result of a seemingly hopeless Colorado trip four months before and an investment of $80. As you may suppose, this financial aspect cuts a small figure when compared with his recovery in this glorious atmosphere of the priceless boon, health. When I left him a few hours ago, with his eyes glistening with tears of gratitude as he dwelt upon this point, I was satisfied that at least one man in Gunnison had indeed "struck it rich." Sands is now in the banking business here and owns half of the best store in the place, as well as a fine lot of real estate here and in the vicinity.

THE SYLVANITE A MINERAL WONDER.

The Sylvanite is located five miles northeast of Gothic on the east side of Silver Mountain, and near the head of Copper Creek. It is 11,700 feet above the sea, and at least 500 feet above "timberline." A chunk of arsenical iron lying among the "drift" or loose rock, nearly 1,000 feet below the present site, first attracted the attention of the Jennings Brothers to the locality, and putting it under a blow-pipe beautiful globules of silver came to the surface. A few hours later (on May 28, 1879), the discovery was made by their simply following the enticing trails of detached masses of "blossom rock" (croppings of the vein) up hill to the source. The wonderfully rugged mountain here seems to culminate in one vast upheaval of brownish iron-stained rock, fabulously rich in silver, and whose limits thus far baffles all attempts at calculation, while hundreds of acres of the precipitous range below are covered with ore and surface stuff representing the crumbling of ages. The vein, if there is one, runs northeast and southwest, and such foreign rock as has been found (I cannot designate it as "wall-rock," as there are no defined walls yet) is mainly metamorphic slate and quartzite. Ore worth

FROM $100 TO $20,000 PER TON

is found in several veins, from inches to 2 feet thick. The entire croppings of this mine, deposit, chimney, or whatever experts will in time call it, protrude from a dozen to 100 feet above the surface proper, and are from 50 to 150 feet wide throughout the entire length of the claim, 1,500 feet. A charred and twisted appearance of the entire mass bespeaks terrific volcanic action. The pay material consists of native silver, sulphurets of silver, ruby silver and traces of horn silver, and the ore thus far shipped has yielded from four to seven-tenths of an ounce of gold per ton. A very little arsenic and sulphur is present, but not a trace of galena, and the ore is practically a "free smelting" product, yielding readily to the more simple formulas known in the art of smelting. The developments are three tunnels, the longest, 100 feet, opening out the ore-body finely at a depth of 70 feet. A shaft is being sunk from the bottom of the main tunnel, 40 feet from the entrance, but has only progressed a few feet.

The Sylvanite shows for at least a thousand feet upon the surface and in all the openings just noted the richest silver ore I have ever seen in large masses, not even excepting the famous Silver Islet vein in the Lake Superior country. While I was at the mine a blast broke down about a ton of ore in the breast of the 100-foot tunnel, and I had the pleasure of seeing four quartz nuggets brought out, and since conveyed hither on the backs of mules and on "slides," all the result of that one blast, which are a small fortune in themselves. No. 1 weighs 600 pounds, and by scientific tests shows a valuation of $4,000 in silver; No. 2 weighs 120 pounds, and contains $950; No. 3 weighs 60 pounds, value $537, and the other, a forty pounder, is as rich as any. These, with 1,000 pounds of other specimens from the Sylvanite, showing silver in all the attractive forms nature has given it, are to go to Chicago, there to be gazed at a few weeks and thence to New York for the special benefit of some of the Leadville operators who have been crying "Gunnison gone." About two tons of ore wheeled out the morning of my visit exhibited

NATIVE AND RUBY SILVER IN EVERY POUND.

Nuggets of pure silver as large as grains of wheat were seen in many places. To regale me in this prosy matter of jotting down hard facts, I have before me one ingot of nearly pure silver weighing a pound and a half, and at the mines sat on two sacks of ore weighing about eighty-five pounds each and containing $800 silver per sack. One shipment of 400 sacks of ore about twelve tons that has been carefully sampled will average $3,500 to the ton. A carload of this class of material will reach the Balbach works at Newark, N. J., about the time this letter appears, and will, according to careful estimate, pan out $40,000. The ore as now assorted from the 22-inch pay streak in the main tunnel, yields as follows: First class, $6,000 to the ton; second class, $2,500; and third class, $75 per ton. The superintendent was just in the midst of the agreeable task of taking out $100,000 worth of ore at an expense, he said, of $16,000, the ore product coming mainly from tunnels, and the latter sum representing his entire expense of sinking, driving tunnels and other "dead work" for this fall.

Thus far the ore has gone mainly to the Pueblo Smelting Works, this State. Freight thither is about $35 per ton, and smelting $75 to $100 per ton. Comfortable houses are being built, and supplies taken to the same to insure steady work all winter at even that great altitude. Some twenty-five men are employed. No great amount of ore will be shipped until a wagon-road is constructed nearer the mine. Only a trail leads there now, and all supplies and ores must be packed five miles up or down a steep grade. Over three thousand feet in altitude is gained in the five miles, and the transportation problem is at present the worst of all. Even water must be carried on mules from a snowbank 500 feet below, and heavy timber a much greater distance. A road can be built, however, at comparatively small cost to within 1,000 feet of the mine, and the plan is to bridge this distance with wire tramway.

THE NEW OWNERS.

The mine is held entirely by men of wealth, who could well afford to make these improvements upon a much poorer guarantee than the Sylvanite gives. Captain James M. Ballentine, for twenty years prominently identified with steamboating enterprises at Chicago, is managing director, Samuel W. Allerton, a millionaire livestock dealer of Chicago, Buffalo, and other points, and T. M. Avery, President of the Elgin Watch Company, with the original purchasers of the Sands interest, already named, are prominent owners. The Jennings Brothers sold out early last fall, realizing enough to enable them to live handsomely anywhere the balance of their days. The mine is capitalized at $4,000,000, divided into 80,000 shares of $50 each. It needs no expert to demonstrate that if the mine maintains its present strength and richness to a depth of even 200 or 300 feet, it is alone enough to turn the attention of the mining world very strongly upon Gunnison. I should add that this company, which is known as the Ruby Silver Mining and Smelting Company, owns a half dozen or more claims adjoining the Sylvanite, their ground measuring 1,500 feet each way, and Jack Haverly owns what he calls the Sylvanite extension, just over the top of the mountain. He has made no developments of note.

OTHER RICH STRIKES.

The Great Western, Catapult, Grey Copper and Indian Girl are prominent silver quartz claims immediately surrounding the Sylvanite. The Grey Copper makes an excellent showing of ore, similar to that in the Sylvanite, and is being placed in fine producing trim by a force of about twenty-five men. In the immediate vicinity is a noteworthy iron deposit, masses of which I found scattered along our trail, that are from 80 to 90 per cent pure iron. While on the subject of iron I will mention that a deposit of vast extent of hematite, called the Mammoth Mine, averaging 41 per cent iron and a trace of gold and silver, is being opened two and a half miles northeast of Gothic. It is a true fissure vein, nearly vertical, and measures from 20 to 3 feet between walls. Its product is to be utilized, partially as a flux and partially for the gold and silver contained, in the smelting works just starting here.

A mile and a half northeast of Gothic is the Virginia silver mine, next to the Sylvanite, probably the best claim in the camp. Messrs. Holmes & Co. are pushing developments upon it with unusual zeal and are really having an easy time of it, as the ore comes out almost as readily as the Leadville sand carbonates, only pick and shovel being called into requisition. The pay vein is exposed by an open cut for 65 feet, averaging 30 inches in thickness, and yielding black and gray sulphurets of silver worth $250 per ton. Two to three tons of ore are taken out daily and the mine is being placed in condition to yield heavily this winter. The claim was recently bought for $10,000, an amount that could easily be produced from it in a week if an effort was made. The lowest grade of ore taken from the Virginia assays 175 ounces silver, and the product could be sorted up to $2,600 to $3,000 per ton. Other good claims in the immediate vicinity might be named, and then in Bunn's Basin,

Silver Queen Basin, Brush Creek and other districts from three to ten miles away are numerous "prospects" yielding grey copper, native and ruby silver. Some interesting developments have been made about five miles east of Gothic, in the vicinity of Washington Gulch, within the past few days. The Luona claim, a quite recent discovery, is producing fine masses of wire and horn silver. A specimen just brought in from the mine, weighing about 10 pounds, consists of heavy wires of native silver, and is valued at $125. The Mammoth, Belsey, Ore Cash and Eureka, in the same locality, have recently changed hands at respectable figures, the Eureka selling at $90,000, and one-fifth of the Belsey for $22,000. The Broad Gauge, another late discovery, is yielding ore that runs 78 ounces silver and 3 ounces gold to the ton, aggregating $162 in value.

THE ROCK CREEK COUNTRY.

Just over the great divide separating the waters of the Gunnison from those of the Roaring Fork of Grand River, and eight miles northwest of Gothic, is the Rock Creek District, in which the quartz discoveries that led to the opening up of the Gunnison country were made in 1872. The famous Whopper Mine is located near Scofield, in the heart of this district. It will be remembered by those who have read my brief history of the Elk Mountain country in *THE WORLD* that the Waite Brothers have been tunneling into Whopper Mountain for some eight years, generally alone, in the heart of this perfect wilderness, and it is largely due to their unconquerable pluck and tenacity that the world is beginning even this soon to learn something of the wonderful wealth of Gunnison. Galena, Crystal, Treasure and Whopper mountains in the Rock Creek district are seamed with large veins of comparatively low-grade but easily smelted galena ore. Mill runs on the High Tide, Whopper and Homestake and other mines whose ore-bodies are from 8 to 25 feet wide average 50 to 67 ounces silver per ton, and assays of assorted ore frequently show a valuation of 300 to 600 ounces. The district really merges into the Gothic belt and covers 75 square miles of country which presents as bright an outlook to the prospector as any region I know of. In fact, this whole country, and from Ruby Camp north to the Roaring Fork of Grand River, a distance of nearly a hundred miles, abounds in entire mountain ranges upon which it is doubtful whether the feet of white men have ever trod. Only the roughest pioneering has been done.

RICH DISCOVERIES WILL BE MADE FOR YEARS TO COME

by miner and novice alike. I am informed that the Waite Brothers received their reward last March, when they sold the Whopper to Philadelphia parties for $140,000. The Terror, nearby, has sold for $42,000, and the Belle of Titusville for $80,000. The Utah, Silver Reef, Schofield and Crystal, and other properties are entitled to that notice which capitalists are pleased to give mines with liberal dump piles of easily reduced fair grade ores. A forty-ton smelter erected by Quincy capitalists, is to start up at Schofield this month, when hundreds of mere "prospects" will be given a chance to show what they contain. Rock Creek also boasts some good copper ores carrying silver. Hitherto there has been no market for ores, except of course for the small proportion of very high grade mineral which would bear transportation 100 miles to the railroad. Two months ago there was only one cabin at Schofield. The boom came, and with it L. Buddee, a shrewd business man of Quincy, Ill., who has sold $50,000 worth of goods in the last six weeks to the hundreds of miners and others who have so suddenly occupied the land.

NEW CARBONATE FIELDS.

Just now there is a genuine stampede from Ruby, Gothic and other camps to the so-called Spring Creek carbonate fields. These are located near the headwaters of Spring Creek, a tributary of Gunnison River, about twenty miles southeast of Gothic. The American Smelting Company, of Leadville, has been quietly working some fifteen men there for several weeks, and a returned Ruby Camp miner (whose loyalty to Ruby would hardly justify a fair statement) says they are finding sand carbonates worth about $30 per ton at a depth of twenty-eight feet. The bed uncovered in the Doctor and Cora Estelle mines is said to be two feet thick and lies between oxide of iron and limestone. Others who are coming in for supplies say the prospects are very flattering; that hundreds of claims have been staked out in the last few days, a town company organized and two or three hundred men arriving daily in the hope of participating in the creation of a second Leadville. The camp is thirty-three miles northeast of Gunnison City, and is easily reached from either that point, Ruby or Gothic. Seven miles this side of Spring Creek is Cement Creek district, in which that most noted of all Rocky Mountain prospectors, Dick Irwin, declares he has uncovered exactly the formation that belongs peculiarly to the great carbonate camp. The carbonates of lime, ochre and porphyry are all there and pretty well adjusted. But the air is full of rumors of strikes; men are leaving stealthily under cover of night, and boastingly, from daylight till dark, horseback and on foot, with the inevitable pick and shovel, many leaving better mines behind than they will ever find, and the country is so new that we may look for this state of things for years.

SOMETHING MORE ABOUT GOTHIC.

Gothic is beautifully located 8,500 feet above the sea at the east base of Gothic Mountain, where Copper Creek joins East River, and has its business eye out for the trade of all the northwestern portion of the Gunnison country. It contains some 1,200 inhabitants, a newspaper, twelve-ton smelter and bank, and a Chicago company is now preparing to erect works for the reduction of ores by chlordizing, a process that is now in operation in Chicago and does such remarkable things as saving from 90 to 98 per cent of the assay value of ores. Copper Creek affords splendid power for such works, falling as it does in large volume 300 feet in less than half a mile in the immediate vicinity of the town. One perpendicular descent of 50 feet, amid massive and quaintly carved vertical buttresses of granite, is a scene of rare beauty. The lower mountains surrounding Gothic are covered with a thick carpet of bunch grass, insuring at least good summer feed for thousands of cattle and sheep, and the higher ranges are clothed with a heavy growth of pine. Game and fish abound, as in all portions of the Gunnison country.

ROCKY MOUNTAIN SURPRISES.

FIFTH LETTER-CAMP WILLARD ON THE COCHETOPA PITKIN AND ASPEN.

PITKIN, COLORADO, Sept. 12th, 1880.

Perhaps no region on earth presents so many singular anomalies as the Rocky Mountains. Our flowers and snowbanks side by side, our bottomless swamps on mountaintops and parched deserts below sea-level, our winters in midsummer and summers in midwinter, and our striking ups and downs financially and physically, are features of which the world has at least a faint idea. But, after ten years of constant observation in this country, I am attracted less by these things than by the instantaneous everyday creation of vast values and superior civilization in these districts furthest distant from centers of commerce and population, by marvellous progress in corners obscure and almost inaccessible, and by wealth sent the world from rugged, sterile heights among eternal snows, where geologists have told us such wealth could not be. It has only been a fortnight since I commenced my Gunnison letters, and half a dozen seemingly important strikes have occurred in the interval in the district covered. Fair carbonate ores on Spring Creek, fifty miles north of Gunnison; gold quartz over in Washington Gulch, rich silver-bearing galena in sight of Gunnison City, and now a tremendous sensation in gold on Cochetopa Creek, are some of these developments which really promise well. Pitkin is twenty-six miles northeast of Gunnison City. The route is first eastward up Tomichi Valley, a dozen miles, to Parlin's ranch, and thence northward fourteen miles along Quartz Creek. Between, Gunnison and Parlin's Cochetopa Creek empties into Tomichi River, and although this letter was intended as a resume of all the northwestern portion of the Gunnison country, with Pitkin as the common center, I will branch off a few minutes on the Cochetopa "find" as a wayside circumstance and one of the "anomalies."

CAMP WILLARD - GENUINE STAMPEDE.

Camp Willard is the name given the Cochetopa diggings. It is fifteen miles southeast of Gunnison, in some low timberless mountain ranges, and not more than 8,500 feet above the sea. There is nothing in the appearance of the surroundings to warrant results now shown; in fact, no less an experienced personage than Jack Haverly's principal prospector, who has been in about all the camps of the Rockies for the past twenty years, says: "If I had caught a man of mine hunting among those Cochetopa hills for gold, I would have helped drum him out of camp." However, a few days ago, a miner came into Gunnison with a piece of white, flinty quartz, sparkling with its wealth of native gold, and said it was from Cochetopa. An assay gave $2,108.34 per ton. The news spread like wildfire, and soon the old stories, handed down from the earliest days of Colorado history, of "pound diggings on the Cochetopa," flashed through a dozen Gunnison camps. In two days some 4,000 people had stampeded to the "find," and at this writing a town is being built, a railroad survey up Cochetopa Creek has been made, claims are recorded by the hundred daily, and about every branch of business is represented. The Lubricator, Maple Leaf, and other claims, have every appearance of true fissure veins, and are traceable by large croppings for hundreds of feet at a stretch. These croppings generally consist of an almost pure white flinty quartz showing a great deal of gold and some copper, but several claims in which silver predominates have also been recorded. I am reliably informed that of the hundreds of assays of gold quartz already made, none have shown less than $100 per ton. The silver ore, all croppings, yields from twenty to fifty ounces silver per ton. Respectable quantities of Lubricator quartz are now being sacked for shipment from an open cut only six feet deep. Assays of this quartz show such fabulous yields as $15,000 and $20,000 per ton. The Cochetopa mineral belt, so far as its boundaries can now be determined, is about ten miles long by five wide, and this area is fairly alive with prospectors. Fair prospects of gold in the sands of the creek have led to extensive preparations for working a number of placer claims.

PITKIN AND VICINITY.

Passing on to Pitkin, we find it located in a beautiful park at the head of Quartz Creek, twenty-six miles northeast of Gunnison, and about fifteen miles west of Hancock, on the Denver, South Park & Pacific Railroad. Its altitude is 9,100 feet above the sea. On three sides high mountains oppose their densely timbered fronts, which are here and there cleft by gulches leading to the extensive mining fields at higher altitudes. Pitkin is a year old, and is entitled to reverence in a region as new as Gunnison. It is, of course, better built than its younger neighbors of which I have been writing, and contains quite substantial and roomy hotels, stores, banks, etc., and about 1,500 residents. With the railroad only some thirty miles away, it has, nevertheless, suffered more through isolation than almost any other mining camp in the Gunnison country. One of the most rugged sections of the Rocky Mountain range lies between it and the railroad, and it has required seventy miles of rough staging to reach it by the roundabout Marshall Pass route. But a stage road has now been completed over Alpine Pass, and the distance shortened more than half, and the Denver, South Park & Pacific Company is piercing Alpine Mountain, ten miles away, with a 2,000-foot tunnel to get its cars into Pitkin early next season. Capital can therefore consider that Pitkin is to be the first railroad town in all this region, and that its interests will bask in the attending boom.

A FIELD FOE THE INEXPERIENCED.

At least a dozen of the large number of mining locations I have examined around Pitkin are veins of great strength and richness. Nearly all are different, however, in one important respect, from those in most other Gunnison camps. The veins rarely show themselves plainly above the surface, being generally covered with from one to ten feet of "slide" or wash gravel. The "float" which guides the experienced prospector to the vicinity of a vein is plentiful enough, but the absence of well-defined croppings must have this result: Mines will be found for years all through the surrounding mountains by the novice and expert alike, merely by stripping surface matter blindly in inviting localities and sinking to a solid formation. So it cannot be said here, as of some districts, that there is no room for prospectors. At whatever depth it has been found thus far, the Pitkin ore in all the mines I have seen has been from fair to very high grade. It is no uncommon thing to find fifteen and twenty foot prospect holes showing veins three to ten feet wide of free milling ores that will yield from $100 to $500 to the ton. Scores of these have from two to ten tons of mineral each ready for shipment. Nearly all the mines thus far produce free milling ores, the product often being gold and silver in about equal proportions. Probably no region outside of the Deadwood belt in the Black Hills is more puzzling to the old miner or exasperating to the "expert" than this, for they find both gold and silver in almost anything, from a sandstone boulder to a mass of petrifaction. In the Little Per Cent and Silver Islet, particularly, I am free to say, geologists will once more find formations whose like were never before seen, enormously rich in gold and silver.

    The first mine to attract attention in the vicinity of Pitkin was discovered a year ago and called the Fairview. It made such a fine showing within twenty feet of the surface that it sold within a few months to Nathaniel Slaght, a Michigan lumberman, for $50,000. It is now 80 feet deep, and a drift at the bottom of the shaft discloses a vein 6 1/2 feet wide. The entire product of this vein averages 150 ounces of silver per ton, and a third of the ore, called first grade, yields from 800 to 1,500 ounces per ton. Near the Fairview, on Fairview Mountain, are the Western Hemisphere, Granite State, Seventy-eight, and others almost as well developed as the Fairview, and yielding just as rich ore. These all carry chlorides and sulphurets of silver and carbonates of lead, and are in a porphyry formation. The Silver Age and Silver Islet are neighboring locations on the same vein. The former was also purchased last fall by Slaght for $40,000. Experts pronounce this:

ONE OF THE MOST WONDERFUL VEINS IN THE ROCKIES.

The Silver Age shaft is down 37 feet, and the Islet 60 feet. Both show the vein of rich milling ore to be from 14 to 16 feet wide. There is so little barren material that the entire product from this enormous crevice will be milled without sorting. About 400 tons of ore, worth some $30,000, are now on the Silver Islet dump. Dr. Tony, of New York City, made careful assays of ore from all parts of this vein at a depth of 25 feet, and found the average value 65 1/2 ounces silver per ton, with a small yield in gold, and at 60 feet the average is 91 ounces silver. At 28 feet the average value of all vein matter in the Silver Age, according to assays by Professor Chisolm, is 184 ounces silver and 2 ounces gold per ton, and at 37 feet two assays just made show 599 and 688 ounces silver. The ore is easily broken in these claims, and considering their great breadth it would seem that production could be made to run up into the hundreds of tons daily with proper development. The Dodson, five miles northwest of Pitkin, is a four-foot fissure vein, carrying free milling ore rich in gold and silver. The main shaft is 75 feet deep, and at its mouth lies 300 tons of ore (mainly the result of sinking this one hole) that will average $100 per ton. The Dodson has produced considerable $500 ore. It was sold when only 25 feet deep to ex-Governor Marshall and Auditor Whitcombe, of Minnesota, and others for $25,000. The Gold Leaf, nearby, is one of the few Pitkin mines which shows above the surface. It has been traced 400 feet by unbroken croppings four feet wide. The pay vein is three feet wide, and the average of ten assays made from different parts of it shows gold and silver to the value of $219 per ton. The Gold Leaf is on Gold Hill, a landmark that is literally seamed from base to summit with similar "prospects," chief among which are the Last Chance, Bertha, Golden Link, Chieftain and Golden Curry. The Golden Link is owned by a Chicago gentleman, who purchased it a few months ago for $15,000, and, in Chicago fashion, has already stocked it at $1,000,000.

Near the head of Armstrong Gulch, two miles away, is the Terrible, whose pay vein of six inches at the surface has steadily increased to twenty inches at the bottom of a 35-foot incline. Surface openings along the vein for 750 feet demonstrate that this is one of the "big things" of the camp. Ore is now being shipped that yields from $100 to $2,000 gold and silver to the ton. The Coal, probably an extension of the Terrible, shows a two-foot pay vein, very rich in chlorides, brittle silver and native gold. A shipment of about two tons, the returns of which have not been received, will, it is believed by those who have handled the ore, yield at least $600 to the ton. The Chloride King has been bonded to Chicago parties for $50,000. Almost every chunk of a lot of five tons of ore at the Terrible at the time of my visit glittered with grains of gold. Three miles down Quartz Creek from Pitkin is the somewhat noted Little Per Cent gold claim which created such a sensation a week or two ago through its $65,000 per ton assay. It has less developments than any of the claims I have mentioned, but has this much of a record: One ton of ore taken as an average from across a three-foot vein yielded $53.

I will add that any of the mines mentioned in this letter can show assays up to almost any figure, because all of them have streaks of wonderfully rich ore, but I have been content to take average yields as a rule to give the intelligent reader a true idea of the value of Pitkin ores. A score or more of such claims as those named should make good shipments of ore within the next sixty days, as the excuse of inaccessibility and high freights can no longer be offered. I believe the Pitkin miners come nearer having a true appreciation of the value of mere prospects than those of any district I have been in, and the reason no doubt is simply that Pitkin has had no boom, and capitalists have not stampeded the prospectors themselves by rushing in and purchasing all sorts of holes at fictitious prices. However, parties are arranging to build a smelter, and others a $100,000 stamp mill, thus insuring at least a small home market for ores, and transportation facilities are rapidly improving, so that possibly the Pitkin prospector will soon have reason to act more like his extravagant friends over at Ruby Camp, Gothic and other lively camps. But at present this is as good as any I know of in Colorado for legitimate investment in mines.

A GOOD SHOW FOR CARBONATES.

This region is probably on the verge of another carbonate sensation. Chicago Park, two and a half miles south of Pitkin, promises strongly to be the scene. A Chicago gentleman has gained a depth there of about fifty feet on each of six shafts, and will continue on the same line all winter, on the strength of indications identical almost with those at Leadville. The lime, iron and porphyry are all there in proper position, and he has struck a large body of decomposed iron, consisting of 10 to 30 ounces silver to the ton. Half a dozen other parties are sinking on claims in Chicago Park, and all are about as jubilant as if they were penetrating the crust of Fryer Hill. The Park is only some 700 feet higher than Pitkin, is in the midst of heavy timber, and has other good natural facilities for the economical working of mines.

Among the important districts in this portion of the Gunnison country is Tomitchi, near the head of Tomitchi River, some 15 miles southeast of Pitkin. The camp numbers over 500 men, and they have uncovered some four or five good lodes, to say nothing of the hundreds of claims which may develop into paying properties when a reasonable amount of work has been put upon them. The belt is from six to eight miles long and about four wide. The ore carries iron pyrites and silver in the form of glance, native and brittle silver. The Little Carry and Brittle Silver locations, both on the same vein, are among the largest ever discovered in Colorado. The crevice is 40 feet wide, and there a pay streak of from five to ten feet. From the San Juan there have been millruns of 90 ounces silver and from the Fort Scott of 100 ounces silver per ton. Senator Hill's smelting works have recently made a run on ore from the Lewiston, with the following result: First class, $607.02 per ton; second class, $421.13 per ton; third class, $112.32 per ton. The Lewiston has a foot of ore that will average $300 per ton, and the Fort Scott two feet of $150 ore. This is one of the very few camps that has commenced shipping ore within a few months after its discovery, and as it will obtain a good start this fall, and the mines can be operated all winter, important developments can be looked for by the time the railroads enter next spring.

HILLERTON MINES AND SMELTERS.

Fifteen miles north of Pitkin, on a spur of the main range known as Fossil Ridge, is the famous Gold Cup group of mines, the Gold, Silver, Iron and Tin Cup and Anna Dietrick being the five principal claims. The Gold Cup and Anna Dietrick are in shape to produce 25 tons of high-grade mineral each daily, and the others can do almost as well. The mines carry both gold and silver, running in value from $200 to $500 per ton. The best smelting works in the Gunnison country are in successful operation on these ores at Hillerton, two or three miles away. The works were completed only a few weeks ago, by C. F. Abbey, of New York, at a cost of $20,000, and are turning out about $1,000 worth of bullion daily.

ROARING FORK AND ASPEN.

Thirty-five miles northwest of Pitkin is the Roaring Fork district, with Aspen as the central camp. The Smuggler and Monarch lead a long list of mines, running high in silver and lead. The mineral of the Monarch protrudes 30 feet from the mountain side, and the vein is over 100 feet wide. Immense boulders of solid galena ore, rich in silver, and weighing hundreds of tons, have become detached from the main body, and lie strewn all over the mountain side below. The Smuggler, however, is considered the great mine of the district. Its width is from 75 to 100 feet, and at the depth of ten feet the ore assays 100 ounces silver and 56 per cent lead. The Spar vein has been traced by its immense croppings, and located for over two miles. It carries copper, stained spar, galena, and sulphurets, assays all the way from $75 to $1,000 having been obtained. Messrs. Breed & Gillespie, of New York, who own several claims on the Spar, are preparing to erect a 100-ton smelter at Aspen.

Recent rich strikes in the Silver Bell, Spar and Pioneer demonstrate that Aspen Mountain is a vast storehouse of mineral. More than 50 mines are being rapidly developed, and at least 20 show extensive bodies of mineral that have obtained mill runs of $100 per ton or more. The contact veins on which so many rich strikes have recently been made are very remarkable for their length, one being located for four miles and two others for about two miles each. The width of the veins varies from 5 to 50 feet. The ore contains no refractory substances, and can easily be reduced at the lowest possible expense when smelters are built at Aspen. The owners of the Spar and Smuggler mines, as well as Messrs. Maxwell & Slater, will each erect smelters early next spring. The Spar and Chloride mines produce ores so rich that they are shipping to Leadville per pack jacks at a cost of $80 per ton. The Spar ore returns as high as $1,000 per ton, and the Chloride from $500 to $2,000. The intrinsic value of the croppings of the Silver Bell are stated to be not less than $50,000. These croppings yield on an average $150 in silver to the ton. The Swedish Boy mine, located on the same vein as the Silver Bell, but two miles south, is producing some wonderfully rich chloride ore that assays over $5,000. The Mother Shifton and Grand Duchess mines, located by two successful English miners and experts, are among the most valuable in the camp. The Mother Shifton shows an immense vein, the croppings of heavy spar and mineral being in places 60 feet wide. It is at present opened by a 30-foot tunnel, showing lime spar and galena in the whole breast. The Grand Duchess has two shafts. No. 1 having five feet of mineral, a fine galena and gray copper, with good hanging wall, the foot wall not yet cut. No. 2 shaft shows six feet of mineral; this No. 2 shaft is 75 feet west of No. 1, and is a distinct vein, thus showing two distinct veins running through these claims and parallel with each other. Assays show 1,500 and 2,400 ounces silver per ton. There were but 500 men in this section this season to prospect a mineral belt 20 miles long, and a very small fraction of a very rich district has been looked over.

ANOTHER SUPERB FIELD FOR SILVER-SEEKERS.

At the head of Castle Creek, 13 miles from Aspen, is the Ashcraft district, which, if anything, presents even better opportunities to the prospector. Many rich strikes have been going on of late, but the first snowstorm of the season has put an end to prospecting. But sufficient development has been made to demonstrate the fact that this is the richest and most extensive mineral belt yet found, with every indication of large veins of free smelting ore, showing ruby and brittle silver, black sulphurets and galena, specimens of which assay into the thousands. Nature has done as much for this country as for any in Colorado. Prospectors will find large mineral outcroppings and mountains covered with float that will enable even the tenderfoot of limited mining knowledge to find the vein without much difficulty. A great rush is expected to this section early in the spring. Ashcraft is 60 miles from Leadville, and the same distance from Buena Vista, and can be reached by wagon road from Buena Vista, which passes directly through the town, or from Leadville, by way of Twin Lakes and Red Mountain pass.

TO PROSPECTOR AND CAPITALIST.

SIXTH LETTER— VAST WEALTH AWAITING APPROPRIATION CLIMATE, AGRICULTURE, ROUTES, RATES, WAGES, ETC.

GUNNISON, COLORADO, September 28, 1880.

In closing this series of letters on the Gunnison country, it affords me pleasure to note that reports now coming in from the various camps at least insure a realization of such hopes as I have from time to time indulged. The Forest Queen mine, at Ruby Camp, has increased its ore shipments to twenty tons daily, worth from $250 to $1,000 per ton. At 65 feet in its main shaft its pay vein is larger and fully as rich as at the sixty-foot point, which I noted in my description of the mine as being an almost unprecedentedly large ore body, considering its fabulous grade. The Bullion King, also in Ruby Camp, has since my notes on it were published, developed a 4-foot vein of ore which, I am reliably informed, will average $850 ounces silver per ton. The Chloride, at Aspen, has recently shown a small vein, having good indications of permanency, that yields ore containing 5,000 to 6,000 silver per ton. New smelters have been contracted for in the last two weeks at Irwin, Aspen and Gothic, and one noted in a previous letter at Hillerton, has been finished and is turning out $2,000 worth of bullion daily. Since making a thorough inspection of the various camps I am satisfied my first estimate of the population of the Gunnison country was much too low. It is easily 18,000 instead of 12,000, as originally noted.

SIX MONTHS' DEVELOPMENT.

The summer has practically been devoted to prospecting. The fall and winter months will show good solid development and a respectable yield of bullion, and, judging from the present yield, the large number of mines being placed in condition to produce and the numerous mills and smelters completed or in progress, it is pretty safe to place Gunnison in 1881 and thenceforth among those Colorado counties which regularly turn out from $1,500,000 to $2,000,000 worth of the precious metals per annum. This is the most conservative view, and is far beneath that which I am willing to admit is among the possibilities. For instance, the Forest Queen can alone produce that amount next year, if put to its trumps, and the Ruby King, at Irwin; Sylvanite, at Gothic; the Silver Age and Islet, at Pitkin, and several others I could mention, can each do half as well, if present appearances go for anything. Or, to outline the possibilities, it should be noted that a section of country, some 3,000 square miles in extent, from Pitkin on the east to Silver Basin on the west, and from Aspen at the north to Camp Willard at the south, is filled with mountain ranges on most of which discoveries of gold or silver-bearing quartz have been made by hundreds, and as a rule the mineral is found in true fissure veins of greater extent and richness on the surface than any in Colorado, or elsewhere that I know of. A drawback in several camps is the refractory nature of the richest ores, but the advent of two railways next year will make the transportation of these to the best smelters of the country a matter of ease and economy.

A SPLENDID FIELD FOR SMELTERS.

This suggests a few words on the reduction of Gunnison ores at home. A successful smelting centre must have in its vicinity, or easily accessible, not only numerous kinds of gold and silver ore, but iron, lead, lime and fuel in abundance. Smelting or reduction works at Denver are eager searchers after the heavy galena ores in one district to use as a flux with richer gold or silver quartz that has been obtained a thousand miles in an opposite direction, and the generally despised low grade iron ore, or the otherwise barely-sought limestone must be had to bring about the proper condition of the mass for successful separation of the precious from the base metals, while fuel for generating the necessary heat is the most important factor of all. Thus it happens that some of our most successful smelting and refining works are furthest from the precious metal supply. Gunnison, for these and other reasons, should be the smelter's Mecca. In the immediate vicinity of Crested Butte, especially, are inexhaustible supplies of iron ore of different grades and natures, from the second-rate "bog" to the richest hematite and magnetic; vast beds of anthracite and coking coal, the former equally as good, and the latter little, if any, inferior to Pennsylvania's best; large areas of dense forests, the only true white pine forests in Colorado outside of San Juan; and superior lime, as well as great and easily utilized water power. I have described the ores in my previous letters, and will only add that about every grade and variety of gold and silver-bearing quartz known in Rocky Mountain mining is found in this region, the common forms in large quantity. The field is not half occupied, considering the mineral now in sight. Following is the present complement: One smelter at Hillerton, 20 tons daily; one 10-stamp mill at Hillerton, capacity about 15 tons; smelter at Crested Butte, capacity 12 tons; smelter at Independence in course of erection, capacity 100 tons; 10-stamp mill at Independence, capacity 15 tons; roaster and mill in Ruby Camp, capacity 15 tons; smelter being built at Irwin, capacity 40 tons; smelter at Schofield, Rock Creek, 20 tons; one smelter completed and another in course of erection at Gothic, capacity of each 20 tons. This gives a total capacity of about 270 tons daily, an amount of ore that the mines of Ruby Camp alone are now producing and next season can easily double.

WHO "PROSPECTS" AND HOW IT IS DONE.

About everybody here prospects or mines, either directly or "by proxy." It is generally considered a science to be followed only by those skilled, but you would be astonished to hear the merchants, the doctors, the lawyers, the preachers, and all the others speculating upon their show for a fortune, in some mines already found, or in one for which they have somebody hunting. Some prominent merchants have three or four prospectors in the field constantly in summer, and it is the best way to acquire mining property if you can find a reliable and experienced man to do the work. In case the merchant or other who "stakes" the prospector desires to own exclusively every claim found, he generally pays $100 wages per month; but if he allows his man to keep, say a one-fourth interest in all he finds, he merely furnishes a "grub stake" of $25 or $30 per month. The latter is much the best plan, because a bare living insured and the chance of making a fortune is a much greater incentive to extra exertion and reliability than merely fair wages a deduction that may be found to apply elsewhere occasionally. A very large proportion of our mines are found in this way. Sometimes, as in the case of Camp Willard, when an unusual sensation is created by rich strikes in the vicinity, the merchant, mechanic or professional man "stampedes" with the rabble, and while he generally comes back with "more experience" and less money than when he started, he sometimes strikes it alongside the old miner. But these classes rarely want anything with a mine except to sell it; and when you do find one working it, he swears he is doing it as a legitimate thing; he wouldn't sell for the world; got the mine to make money out of it; when he knows away down in his ten per cent consciousness that he never dreamed of mining when he "staked" the finder. It is a mistaken notion that old-timers who have been hunting quartz a dozen years or more, make most of the valuable discoveries in an absolutely new country like Gunnison. They are very apt to come from other mining regions and apply rules with the positiveness which characterizes the man who thinks he knows all about some intricate science, and in the vernacular of the country, "get left" by the tenderfoot novice who, far from home and friends and down to his last dollar, is not only possessed with a type of desperation and determination which the old prospector deems unnecessary in his business, but whose head is clear of all hobbies or set rules, and will take right hold anywhere and everywhere to turn up something. Then when he does find a good prospect he will be more apt to sell for a reasonable price instead of spoiling the sale entirely by asking a fortune.

NEWCOMERS HAVE MADE THE STRIKES.

The discoverers of some of the best mines in this country were newcomers. The Forest Queen, for instance, was located by a Marylander who had never seen a mine before, and who had just arrived the night before from his native heath by ox-team, of which he was engineer. He sensibly pocketed $50,000, went his way rejoicing, and was called a fool because his find has turned out to be a $2,000,000 bonanza. Over 6,000 mines have been located in the Gunnison country, and probably not less than three-fourths of the number were easily found by surface croppings which any novice could trace. Several thousand sales have been made, and all of prospects from 10 to 50 feet deep. To show that some one has already made money here with comparatively slight exertion, and that men of money have confidence in the wealth of the country, I will quote a few transfers: Dodson Mine, near Pitkin, $25,000; Whopper, on Rock Creek, $140,000; Forest Queen, Irwin, $40,000; Belle of Titusville, Rock Creek, $60,000; Bullion King and Monte Cristo, Irwin, $105,000; Lead Chief and Independence, Irwin, $100,000 and $120,000 respectively; Fairview, Pitkin, $40,000; Ruby King, Irwin, $50,000. While old prospectors have, as a rule, put a very high valuation upon their finds, the purchasers have on the other hand been very moderate in their capitalization upon forming stock companies. As instances, the Forest Queen, of Irwin, or Sylvanite, of Gothic, each producing their thousands daily, and having millions in sight, would at Leadville or on the Pacific coast have been stocked at not less than $20,000,000 each, instead of $1,000,000 and $4,000,000 respectively.

CLIMATE—STOCK-RAISING.

Gunnison is pre-eminently a mining country, and, as indicated in a previous letter, will not afford many more desirable homes for farmers. The average altitude is great, probably 8,000 feet above the sea the area falling below 7,000 feet, and in which hardy grain and vegetables can be produced with tolerable regularity, being a very small proportion say one tenth of the whole. Weather records are almost wholly lacking, so that the climate, even of that portion that has been inhabited for several years, cannot be treated of with much satisfaction. In the course of many interviews with the oldest settlers I have gleaned these facts: Summer days are generally clear, electric, invigorating, and the nights are always cool; summer temperature 60 to 75. In 1877 there was no winter in the valleys, but a succession of beautiful Indian summer days, up to Christmas. A foot of snow fell during the last days of December, which remained on the ground nearly a month. There was no other snowfall worth noting during the winter. Mercury sank to 26 degrees below zero in January, remained at or below zero for days at a time; but the few herds of cattle then in the country wintered without loss, and received no shelter or food save that obtained by themselves among the hills. In 1878 the weather was exceedingly mild until December, and there was not enough snow in the valleys to afford a week's sleighing during the entire winter. Mercury was lowest 24 degrees below zero in January. Cattle wintered well without hay. This winter, like the previous one, "broke up" in April.

In 1879 snow commenced falling November 20, and for several weeks there were storms almost daily which blockaded the roads and covered the pastures so that the cattle were compelled to feed on willows. The snow was three feet deep in Ohio and Gunnison valleys in December, and receded but little until April. Mercury remained at or below zero during January, and fell to 36 and 40 degrees below at various points. Many cattle, not less than 10 percent of all in the Gunnison country died, as no provision had been made for their care. In 1878 there were showers in summer almost daily, but in 1879 and 1880 the growing seasons were so dry that irrigation had to be practiced, as elsewhere on the Rocky Mountain plateau. In the lower or western half of Gunnison county are several million acres of winter and summer pasturage, which would easily sustain 50,000 head of cattle. That section will be thrown open to settlement by the terms of the treaty now in progress with the Utes.

AGRICULTURE—WHAT FARMERS HAVE DONE.

Frosts are not uncommon in the valleys as late in the spring as June 1, and as early in the fall as September 1. Nevertheless,

Chas. G. Tinguely, who owns a ranch in the Ohio valley, three miles from Gunnison City, has produced fine crops of barley, oats, potatoes and other hardy vegetables, during six successive seasons. John T. Parlin, who has a splendid dairy farm in Tomitchi Valley, twelve miles from Gunnison, has had the same success for the past three years, and I could quote others who have made small fortunes, especially on oats and potatoes, the past two seasons. Wheat is being produced in a small way. Hay, however, is the product of the valleys for profit since mining has necessitated the employment of so many animals. Three years ago this commodity went begging at $5 per ton, and ranches were a drag on the market at $5 per acre. Now I see single loads of hay selling almost any day at $85, and a good hay ranch readily sells for from $30 to $50 per acre. An acquaintance of mine named Mergelman, whom many Denverites remember as a poor clerk in a toy store in that city three years ago, now has 320 acres of hay land, some twelve miles south of here, which nets him from $50 to $75 per acre each season. Last season he sold about 200 tons on the premises for $85 per ton; the prospects are that he will get $100 per ton this winter. His land cost him practically nothing, as he homesteaded and pre-empted it.

It is a mystery how so many of the tame grasses, such as red top, timothy and blue grass, took root in the various valleys, as they were all found here by the earliest known pioneers. As for the flora of the parks and mountains, it surpasses in richness and variety that of our eastern States. Hundreds of the most beautiful and delicately colored varieties are new to the denizen of the East, but he will find all such old friends as the columbine, violet, rose, bluebell, verbena, larkspur, harebell, daisy, astor and buttercup greeting him on every hand.

VALLEYS, PRICES OF PRODUCE, ETC.

The principal valleys are the Gunnison, Tomitchi and Ohio. The two first-named each afford an arable strip of about 30 miles in length by one mile in width, while the Ohio Valley is about 20 miles long and a mile wide. Each of these will still furnish room for a few dozen first-class ranches, and their small tributaries also afford a few cozy nooks for the incoming farmer. Higher up these valleys, and in many little mountain parks are good locations for dairymen, where cattle could obtain splendid pasturage for eight months in the year, but would have to be fed during the other four, and where the climate is too rigorous to admit of the cultivation of the soil.

All the pine, spruce and cedar timber that may ever be required here for building, mining or fencing purposes, will be found on the many mountain ranges, and one cannot go amiss of clear, dashing streams and beautiful lakes. I should add that most of the good hay lands on river and creek bottoms are claimed, but the more extensive bench lands overlooking them, which, after being irrigated one or two seasons without seeding, will produce from one to one and a half tons of superior hay per acre, are nearly all open to entry. The bench lands are more desirable for agricultural purposes than the bottoms, as they are less liable to frosts, and the latter are taken first only because irrigation is not necessary to produce hay upon them. From one to two miles of irrigating ditch, costing from $100 to $150 per mile, will cover claims of the average elevation on the "first benches." The few who take possession of Gunnison's arable area will indeed "strike it rich," for the market furnished by the miner will always be the best in the world, and the prairies of Kansas and Nebraska are too far away to ever compete with the resident farmer, even with rail communication. Oats are now quoted at $6.50 per 100 pounds; potatoes, $3 per 100 pounds; all such vegetables as cabbage, beans, beets, turnips, etc., from $6 to $12 per 100 pounds; butter, 50 cents per pound; eggs, 40 to 50 cents per dozen.

MONEY IN REAL ESTATE.

I have in a previous letter ventured some suggestions to capitalists or men of moderate means concerning Gunnison mining camps as desirable fields for investment, but I believe only allusion has been made to operations in real estate, to merchandising or manufacturing. There will be four or five good solid towns in Gunnison towns possessing in two or three years from 3,000 to 7,000 permanent residents each. The bulk of the money has probably already been made on Gunnison town lots, but thousands of dollars are yet to be made, and those who arrive this fall or early next spring will do the gleaning. Jim Kelley, an old government herder, located half of the present townsite of Gunnison a year ago, at an expense of $1.25 per acre. In May of the present year, he sold his interest to Jack Haverly and associates for $30,000. Haverly was called foolish, and Gunnison property has month by month been called too high, but it continues to advance, and men who purchased lots from Haverly three months ago for a few hundred dollars now hold at a thousand, and the end is not yet. Less than a year ago, a few miners organized the town of Irwin, in Ruby camp, and sold lots at $10 each. Those same lots sell readily now for $500 to $1,500 each, and from present prospects will double in value inside of the next year. Pitkin, Gothic, Crested Butte, and other points whose foundations are gold and silver, are undergoing the same experience, and call it extravagance, "mushroom growth," or what you will, these fissure-vein mining camps will furnish as many examples of suddenly acquired wealth in real estate speculation in their business centers as in the mines themselves. Gunnison ranch property is also worth looking after. Unsettled and unimproved tracts, now to be had for the simple taking, so limited in extent, located in sight of rich and populous mineral districts, and easily rendered productive, are worth intrinsically more, acre for acre, than the gardens of Long Island, simply because their productions will always sell for double, triple or quadruple the price ever realized from those of the latter.

SOME OF GUNNISON'S NEEDS.

Small foundries or machine shops are needed sadly in Irwin, Gothic and Gunnison, and a lucrative business awaits a good hotel man in three or four of the best towns. Irwin, Gothic, Pitkin, and several other points, each need good stock of furniture and a good stationery house. Dealers in mining and milling machinery would find it profitable to survey this entire field. There are plenty of good clothing, grocery and dry-goods houses, but one or two more hardware establishments could find locations. There is but one good planing mill in the country, and three or four will doubtless find desirable openings next spring. Goods in all lines must be first-class in this country. The best prices are readily obtainable for them, while cheap and shoddy wares can hardly be given away. As an illustration of what a little capital backed with plenty of energy and good judgment will do in a new country, I will mention the case of some acquaintances here and it is only one of dozens that have come to my notice on my trip. Two young gentlemen last June bought a stock of general merchandise, which invoiced $11,000, paying $1,800 in cash and agreeing to give one-half the receipts each day until the remaining $9,200 was paid. The entire amount was paid in six weeks and the firm is now one of the best in Gunnison; it will pay $10,000 for freight this season.

Business is done on a cash basis, and it is one of the very few countries in which people seem to buy things only when they have the money in their pockets to pay. This season, although a generally prosperous one for the merchant, is for certain reasons less lively than succeeding ones will doubtless be. Prospectors and others who came into the country early in the summer almost invariably brought loads of supplies with them, because it was generally believed that no adequate supply of goods were here, or would be until very late. Thus it has happened that goods have often been sold by the wagon load on the streets for what they would bring. Business is now settled, Gunnison is no longer a wilderness and the Gunnison merchant will hereafter get what rightfully belongs to him. Rents of business houses vary but little in the different towns. One floor, say 25x75 feet, $75 to $100 per month; shops or smaller houses, $40 to $60. Freights on merchandise from Chicago or St. Louis to Gunnison, 3 to 4 cents per pound; from Denver, 2 to 2-1/2 cents. Insurance is obtainable only at heavy premiums on account of the large preponderance of frame buildings, but this is constantly improving as the flimsy structures are gradually giving way to those of brick and stone. Interest on loans, 1-1/2 to 3 per cent per month. Banking facilities are first-class, the Bank of Gunnison, located here, having for its backers such men as Governor Tabor and for its manager Colonel Sam. G. Gill, for many years prominently identified with that colossal Western institution, the First National, of Denver.

EMPLOYMENT AND WAGES.

It is a frequent remark just now throughout the country that Gunnison is full of men out of employment. To some extent the charge is true. But the trouble lays with the men, not with the country. Those who are idle are as a rule the class who sit beside the stove of some saloon looking for work. I have investigated this matter very closely, and while I have occasionally found men walking towards the Atlantic cursing the country, I have more often found employers keenly on the watch for reliable help. I will go so far as to say I don't believe there is a man in the Gunnison country today who need be idle forty-eight hours if he is willing to roll up his sleeves and take hold of good, healthy manual labor at anything that presents itself. It is like many other things in a new country; for instance, you will meet half a dozen men on the way out of Gunnison, swearing there is not a good mining property in it, and you will meet another half dozen who can show the nice little homestake of hard cash they have just received for a mine. Mechanics and thorough miners are more in demand than laborers, and house servants more than all other classes combined. Following are average wages at present: Carpenters, $3.60 per day; bricklayers, masons and plasterers, $5 per day; blacksmiths, $4 per day; laborers, $2.50 per day: house servants, $25 per month and board; hotel waiters, $25 per month: cooks, $75 per month; teamsters, $30 per month and board; tinners, $3.50 per day.

LIVING EXPENSES, BUILDING MATERIAL, ETC.

Thousands will come to Gunnison next year, and they should have an idea before starting of what living expenses will be in their new home. Following are figures that rule just now, and it is just to say that the two railways which will penetrate Gunnison next year, will, before any considerable influx can occur, have the effect of cheapening many items materially: Flour, $6.50 to $7.25 per 100 pounds; corn meal, $6; sugar-cured hams, 18 cents per pound; lard, 18 cents; butter, 50 cents; granulated sugar, 18 cents; coffee "A" sugar, 17 1/2 cents; dried fruits 20 to 30 cents; coffee, green, 25 to

30 cents; tea, 80 cents to $1.60; fruits and vegetables, two-pound cans, 30 to 35 cents; all fresh vegetables, 8 to 10 cents per pound; chickens, $10 to $12 per dozen; milk, 10 cents per quart; steaks, 15 to 20 cents per pound; roasts, 12 to 15; venison, elk and bear, 10 to 15; mountain trout, 30 to 40 cents per pound; day board, $5.50 to $10 per week; board and lodgings, $10 to $20. Rents of three and four-room cottages, $18 to $25 per month; livery, double-seated carriage, $8 per day; single seat, $5; riding horses, $4; boarding horses at stables, $4 per team per day; dressed lumber, $40 to $50, and rough lumber, $30 to $40 per 1,000 feet; shingles, $5.50 per 1,000; bricks, $10 to $12 per 1,000; superb building stone, $1.25 per perch.

ROUTES, RATES, DISTANCES AND TOLLS.

How to get here and the cost, as well as the facilities for travel in the Gunnison country, are questions no doubt daily asked in the outside world. Gunnison is as easily reached as was Leadville a year ago, and railways are approaching so rapidly that the travel of another season will mainly come by rail right to this site of the principal Ute camp of a year ago. From the Eastern seaboard to the Missouri River in these days of elaborate railway advertising the route is plain, and thence to Denver one cannot well go amiss. If the traveller reaches the Missouri at Kansas City or Leavenworth he takes the old Kansas Pacific line; if he comes by the more northerly belt and lands at Omaha, the Union Pacific is the open sesame. By either of these routes he comes from the Missouri River to Denver in about thirty-one hours; there connecting with trains of either the Denver, South Park and Pacific, or Denver and Rio Grande railways, he journeys through some of Colorado's grandest scenery some ten hours to those common points, Alpine (present terminus D., S. P. & P. Railway), and Poncha Springs (on the D. & R. G. Railway), from where Concord coaches of the Sanderson line convey him through to Gunnison City in ten or twelve hours more. Time from either Kansas City, Leavenworth or Omaha to Gunnison, about fifty-one hours; fares from either of these points rule about as follows: To Gunnison or Pitkin, first-class, $46.70; emigrant (which on these lines means second-class passage on express trains), $39.70; to

Irwin, Ruby Camp and Gothic, first-class, $52.70; emigrant, $45.70. Holders of emigrant tickets on the Kansas and Union Pacific line allowed 150 to 200 pounds of baggage free.

From Gunnison there are daily stage lines to Irwin, Gothic, Crested Butte, Pitkin, and all other prominent points. Distances and rates from Gunnison are as follows: Irwin, Ruby Camp, 30 miles, fare $6; to Crested Butte, 27 miles, fare $4; to Gothic, 36 miles, fare $5; to Pitkin, 26 miles, fare $4; to Ohio City, 18 miles, $3.25; to Jack's Cabin, 17 miles, fare $2.50; to Lake City, 60 miles, $8.50; to Ouray, 110 miles, $16.50. It may interest those who are coming in conveyances of their own to know that nearly all roads in the Gunnison country are toll roads, and that the tolls for each ten miles will average about as follows: For two-horse team and wagon, $1; each additional team, 50 cents; saddle animals, 25 cents; one horse and carriage, 50 cents. Occasionally we strike a toll bridge, or rather the toll bridge strikes us with wonderment when the rates are announced, which are all the way from 10 cents for a footman to $1 for teams. A bridge costing $500, across the Gunnison River near here, has had average receipts of $65 per day all this summer.

POPULATION, VALUATION, HEALTHFULNESS.

Among the many items which suggest themselves as I close are those relating to valuation, population, society, healthfulness, &c. The permanent towns, whose sites one year ago were hardly marked by a single cabin, are Gunnison, population 2,000; Aspen, 1,000; Pitkin, 1,500; Willard, 2,500; Irwin, 3,000; Gothic, 1,000; Schofield, 800; Tomitchi, 500; Spring Creek, 600; Independence, 500. Schools, churches, libraries, and secret societies are being established in all of these. The assessed valuation of Gunnison county one year ago was about $130,000 and is now about $1,000,000. The Gunnison or Elk Mountain country at all times and places presenting a magnificent landscape, its mountains fairly ribbed with gold, silver, iron and coal and its valleys fertile and traversed by streams alive with trout, its forests abounding in noble game, its climate rigorous but healthful to the end, and its geology a law and mystery unto itself, is surely an inviting field for wasting energy or capital, for the scientist and the devotee of rod and gun.

SAN JUAN.

THE HOME OF TRUE FISSURE VEINS LAKE, GALENA, ANIMAS, OURAY, SAN MIGUEL, SILVERTON, RICO, AND OTHER DISTRICTS.

Adjoining the Gunnison country on the south is the vast mountain region of San Juan, soon to be known as one of the greatest silver producers in the world. It occupies 15,000 square miles of Southwestern Colorado a region greater in extent than either New Jersey, New Hampshire or Vermont, with Delaware thrown in and, like its northern neighbor, it is composed of a series of the most stupendous mountain ranges in the world. As one writer has expressed it, "There is probably more country standing on edge in this section than any where else beneath the sun." These mountains contain thousands of silver veins, many of huge size and some of great richness. In fact, well informed miners and geologists tell us that they present a greater number of true fissure mineral veins, easily traceable upon their towering fronts and summits, than any known region of similar extent on the globe. The silver belt is from 30 to 40 miles wide and nearly 100 miles long. It has taken years to build a few roads through this rugged and almost impassable country, and the heavy snows and long winters have also been a serious drawback to growth and development. It has been a quite recent thing to attempt to mine there in winter except in running a few tunnels, but the rapid approach of the Denver, South Park Pacific and Denver & Rio Grande Railways is changing the whole face of things.

Access is now comparatively easy, smelters are being built, and a market is being created for ores, which, though classed high grade, were until the present almost worthless, because transportation and reduction consumed their value. So we may confidently look for great developments in San Juan during 1881. Up to 1880 the entire silver and gold yield of the region was $1,501,000; it has single mines which, with proper development, should yield that amount annually. With the exception of those in one or two small districts, which are rich in gold, its ores are principally galena, carrying silver in the form of "ruby," "sulphurets," "gray copper" and "native." The veins are not as conspicuous for their great size as those of Gunnison (usually ranging from 1 to 3 feet in width), but for their great length, their continuous fair average grade, and, as already noted, the wonderful frequency of their occurrence in various formations.

SUMMIT DISTRICT.

Commencing with the eastern edge of San Juan, we first encounter Summit Gold Mining District, which has been made famous principally by the Little Annie and Golden Queen claims. The former has yielded about $500,000, its product being worked in a small 10-stamp mill, and the latter has recently been producing several thousand dollars per week. Many tons of the rich, decomposed quartz of these mines have yielded from $500 to $1,000 per ton, and at different times during the past five years Summit Mountains have been the scene of wild stampedes on account of oft-recurring strikes of "pockets" in these and other properties which literally sparkled with their wealth of native gold. But the Summit Hills have been pretty well prospected, and to my mind the brightest field in San Juan for either capitalist or prospector is in the silver districts farther west.

LAKE DISTRICT,

in the northern central portion of San Juan is one of these. It contains nearly 1,000 located veins, most of them silver, a few very rich in gold, and has thus far furnished the bulk of southwestern Colorado's bullion output. On the mountains bordering Hensen Creek are some of the most noted lodes. Five miles from Lake City are the Ute and Ule, the former having from 5 to 7 feet of solid mineral, and the latter nearly as much. These great veins yield from $10 to $500 silver per ton, $30 or $40 in lead and from $3 to $10 in gold. Their yield in 1879 and 1880 was about $225,000. The Belle of the West, in the same district, shows from 6 inches to 2 feet of ore which averages over $100 per ton.

The mines on the Lake Fork of the Gunnison are admirably located near the valley, cutting the mountains at right angles, so that tunnels can be driven in on them. Thus expensive shafts and crosscut tunnels are unnecessary. Among them the Hotchkiss is probably the most noted, having a tremendous vein of some 7 feet in width and yielding some very high grade telurium ore. An exciting gold discovery was made on Gold Hill, only a few miles above Lake City, recently, and another along the Cimmaron, 18 miles away, on ground which prospectors have roamed over for years. It shows that there is plenty of room for the prospector. There are some 70 mines, all of which show good ore bodies, being actively developed in Lake District. Many more are worked to some extent, and the mountains are practically worked. There are several smelting establishments in the district, the Crooke Works at Lake City being the most extensive and successful.

PARK DISTRICT AND ENGINEER MOUNTAIN.

Near the head of Henson Creek, about 20 miles from Lake City, at an altitude of 13,000 feet, are the Inez and other prominent mines of Park District. The Inez has produced many tons of decomposed sulphurets worth $150 per ton. The Palmetto mine, on the northern slope of Engineer Mountain, is one of the budding bonanzas of San Juan. It has produced ore in 40-ton lots which sold for from $200 to $450 per ton. It shows a vein from 12 to 24 inches wide, carrying ruby, brittle and wire silver. Hoisting and reduction works are being erected by the Palmetto Company and the bullion output for 1881 will undoubtedly be a heavy one. The Mammoth, a neighboring claim, shows 4 feet 8 inches of good smelting ore, whose average mill runs are: First-class, $1,200 to $1,500 per ton;

second-class, 277 ounces silver and 3 ounces gold; third-class, 119 ounces silver and 1 1/2 ounces gold. Sample tests for sorting on the dump show: First-class, from $2,000 to $3,500 silver and $80 gold; second-class, 1,040 and 820 ounces silver and 3 ounces gold; third-class, 277 ounces silver and 2 6-10 ounces gold, and 189 ounces silver and 1 ounce gold. The Polar Star is also a mine of high local reputation.

ANIMAS FORKS.

Animas Forks, situated at the confluences of the North and West forks of the Animas River, some 27 miles southeast of Lake City, is the center of a large mining region, comprising Poughkeepsie Placer and California gulches on the north and west, and Burns' and Picayune gulches on the south. It is surrounded by lofty mountain peaks on every side, and in whatever direction the eye of the observer may be turned the work of the miner and capitalist can be seen.

The concentration works of Greenleaf & Co. are located here, while Professor Jas. A. Cherry has built a 10-ton smelter just below the town. He is backed by Chicago capital, and will obtain ore enough from the Red Cross, Eclipse and other mines of his company to supply the smelter.

Prof. Cherry informs us that the Red Cross shows four feet of solid galena carrying gray copper. It opened with ore running less than eight ounces and will now average over 160, while selected ores assay 1,300. The Eclipse is a lower extension of the famous Mountain Queen, at the head of the left fork of the Animas. It shows 10 feet of solid galena carrying gray copper and brittle silver, which the Professor says will average 60 ounces silver. There are five well defined pay-streaks in the vein. The Maid of the Mist, Red Cloud, Mastodon and Boston are all rich mines in the vicinity of Animas Forks. The Ashtabula pay vein is two feet wide. Several veins in this district have been traced from one to two miles on the surface.

SILVERTON AND SURROUNDING DISTRICTS.

About 40 miles southwest of Lake City, in Baker's Park, and in the center of the San Juan mineral belt is Silverton. On Hazelton

Mountain, which slopes almost to the edge of the town site, are situated the Aspen, the Susquehanna, Prospector, Gray Eagle and McGregor, as well as many other mines which have produced ore for the market. On Sultan Mountain, which joins its southern boundary, are the North Star, Empire, Ajax, Belcher and Jennie Parker, all producing mines, with many more equally good awaiting development by cross-cut tunnels to make them add to the volume of mineral wealth to be brought here for ultimate market from that mountain. On Kendall and King Solomon Mountains are also many veins rich in silver and lead. The same is true of the surrounding mountains for a dozen miles in all directions, every one of which is scarred with a network of fissure veins bearing silver.

The Aspen, on Hazleton Mountain, has yielded over 1,000 tons of ore which, in Green & Co.'s Silverton smelter, averaged 114 ounces silver per ton and 60 percent lead. The Susquehanna, on the same mountain, has had about 200 tons of ore smelted which averaged $160 silver per ton and 60 percent lead. It has yielded ore worth $1,200 per ton. On silver-ribbed King Solomon Mountain are many veins traceable for miles by great croppings on the surface. The North Star is 40 feet in width and has been traced for three miles. The ores are argentiferous galena, gray copper and yellow sulphide of copper, containing from 40 to 400 ounces silver per ton and 60 to 65 percent lead. The product for recent years has averaged $155 per ton silver besides the lead. The Highland Mary is also a noted mine. Near the base of Sultan Mountain is the North Star, whose value may be judged from the fact that one-half of a six months lease on it has been sold for $10,000. It has something like 2,000 tons of ore on the dump, worth an even $200,000, and it is believed it could alone supply a small smelter with ore year after year. The Cleveland, an adjoining claim on Sultan Mountain, has yielded small lots of ore, averaging 600 ounces silver per ton. The Denver & Rio Grande Railway will probably reach Silverton during autumn of 1881.

Eureka, seven miles above Silverton, on the Animas River, is surrounded by towering mountains, where galena veins crop out on the surface in a remarkable manner. The Niagara Consolidated Mining and Reduction Company, under the able management of Prof. Theo. B. Comstock, is delving into the depths from the summit of Niagara Mountain, unearthing and utilizing a rich body of mineral.

THE MINES OF POUGHKEEPSIE GULCH

lie just over the crest of the Uncompaghre Mountain, 20 miles north from the Silverton country. The mines are about the head waters of the Uncompaghre River, that flows north into the Gunnison, and its numerous tributaries coming down from the mountain heights on the south and west. The district really extends down from the mountains to the north, merging into that surrounding Ouray. The mountain sides all along and all through this extent, are thickly seamed with silver lodes that show assays of from one to two thousand dollars.

In the Poughkeepsie Gulch region are such noted silver mines as the Saxon, yielding ores worth $1,700 to the ton; the Alaska, $997; the Poughkeepsie, $95; Bonanza, $125; the Red Rogue, Adelphi and others, all producing rich ores. The mountains surrounding Poughkeepsie Gulch are exceedingly rough, and will be a good field for the prospector ten years hence at present rate of development.

OURAY, MOUNT SNEFFLES AND SAN MIGUEL.

Ouray is the center of a vast area of rich mineral country in the northwestern portion of San Juan. It is reached from the south via Silverton, or from the north via Gunnison City. Mount Sneffles is the most important district in the vicinity. It embraces all the mines located up Cañon Creek and on Potosi Mountain, Ruby Mountain, Stony Point, Sneffles Basin, Imogene Basins and Virginius Basin, and they include some of the richest mines in the San Juan. Passing up Cañon Creek to Mount Sneffles, the first important piece of property is the Mineral Farm, comprising four locations and being really forty acres of solid mineral digging, which several years ago sold for $75,000. Any portion of this forty acres will expose mineral in paying condition from the very grass roots.

Near by is the Virginius mine, which has produced during the past two years large quantities of high grade ore, and has recently been sold by C. C. Alvord, of Denver, for the comfortable sum of $100,000. Its ores have averaged nearly $400 per ton. The Terrible, located in the same basin with the Virginius, has also recently been sold for $50,000. The Smuggler, owned by Ingraham & Ohlwiler, stands out as one of the richest mines in the State, producing both gold and silver in large quantities.

On what is known as Ruby Mountain there are located such well-known mines as the Wheel of Fortune, Silver Queen, Monetizer, Grand Trunk and Mark Twain. These mines are owned by a company with Governor Hoyt, of Pennsylvania, at its head. The Hoosier Girl, Pocahontas, Crusader, Gertrude, Talisman, U. S. Deposit, Richmond, Hidden Treasure, Security, Revenue, Declaration, First National, Saracen and Imogene, are also located on Ruby Mountain and in the Imogene Basin, all being very valuable pieces of property, upon which development is being systematically pushed. The Hidden Treasure has an 18-inch vein of gray copper, which, in the smelting works, has averaged about $200 per ton.

San Miguel district occupies a tract of country 40 miles broad by some 65 miles long, and located just west of Ouray and Mount Sneffles. All along San Miguel Creek for nearly 70 miles are rich placer diggings, some of which are being operated on an extensive scale with hydraulics. The Wheeler & Kimball claim, consisting of 400 acres, yields an average of 50 cents to the cubic yard. The "Kansas City" claim has several million yards of ground, estimated from tests to average $1 per yard. San Miguel gold is worth $17.50 per ounce. About $75,000 have recently been expended in constructing flumes and ditches to cover claims along this creek, and from this one yields are expected to be enormous. There is still field for investment well worth the attention of mining capitalists.

THE CARBONATES OF DOLORES.

The Dolores country is about 70 miles southwest of Ouray, or 45 miles northwest of the new Denver & Rio Grande railway town of Durango. It is rapidly coming to the front as a carbonate district, and an expert goes so far as to say: Rico will be a second Leadville, in all that expression implies. Within a radius of two miles of Rico there are at present, open and paying, two carbonate mines for every one which Leadville could boast of eighteen months ago. The formation is the exact counterpart of that of the Leadville district, the contact of limestone and porphyry being perfect, the limestone forming the footwall, and the porphyry the hanging walls of veins or deposits of ore which are capped in many instances with iron. The veins or deposits vary in width from a few inches to over 20 feet. The exact similarity of the Rico ores to those of the Leadville district has been most satisfactorily and fully demonstrated; all of the various characters of carbonate ores having been found in abundance, including hard and soft sand and gray carbonates. There are at present in the camp at least 50 paying carbonate mines, as a result of the work of discovery and development, covering a period of a few months. When I say paying mines, I mean mines the ores from which will stand $65 for transportation, $20 for treatment, and leave a handsome margin of profit to the producers.

With smelting works, cheap transportation, and cheap fuel, at least 100 properties will be immediately added to the paying list. The mines which will thus be made paying properties are similar to those from which at Leadville, at the present time, the great bulk of her mineral production comes from mines which produce from 5 to 200 tons of ore per day, which will run from 20 to 100 ounces in silver per ton. In all these properties, unproductive and unprofitable today, which are owned by poor men, and which can be bought for from $5,000 to $50,000, there is a golden opportunity for the capitalists. Such an opportunity for safe investments, guaranteeing immense profits, is not presented by business enterprises of any kind in any part of the world. Here again, to illustrate, I must hazard my prophetical reputation, to-wit: The $5,000 to $50,000 mining properties of today will be more readily sold in 13 months' time at prices ranging from $50,000 to $5,000,000. The Dolores Carbonate Camp has been examined by many of the most eminent geologists and mining experts in this country, and I have yet to hear of one who has not given the most flattering reports of its extensive wealth and resources in carbonate ores. The most prominent mines, as far as yet opened and at present worked, are the Grand View, Alma Mater, Little Jim, Cross, Hope, the Bertha with a 12-foot pay streak running well in gold as well as high in silver, Pelican, Yellow Jacket, Glasgow with 15 feet of pay ore, Ethlena, Gertie, Democrat, Edith, Melvina, Pigeon and Wabash, on Telescope Mountain (Nigger Baby Hill), from half to one mile and a half from Rico; the Newman, Rico Muldoon, Black Demon, O. G. Marston and Little Annie, on Dolores Mountain; the Puzzle, Lucky, Highland Mary, Lady Elgin, Little Susie, Elgin Boy, Little Carrie and St. Louis, on Expectation Mountain; from all of the above mines, mill runs from 75 to 1,000 ounces in silver to the ton have been obtained, while from at least 10 of these mill-runs, in lots from three to 20 tons, have given from 250 to 1,000 ounces in silver to the ton.

LA PLATA COUNTY AND DURANGO.

La Plata county is in the extreme southwestern corner of Colorado, and is just now attracting more attention than any other portion of San Juan, because it has assurance of railway communication (Denver & Rio Grande) early in the summer of 1881.

Already a wild stampede is setting in to the new town of Durango, near Animas City, at the eastern edge of the county. New mines are being discovered in surrounding mountains, ranches taken up in neighboring valleys, and a large smelter is being erected on the new town site. While mines of silver and gold are numerous and rich, the coal fields are generally considered most important. The area of coal land is estimated at nearly 1,000 square miles. The La Plata coal bed has an extreme thickness of 50 feet, and contains about 40 feet of good coal, free from slate. There are other beds running in thickness from 10 to 20 feet, and altogether these are among the largest and best deposits of semi-bituminous coking coal in the world.

La Plata county bids fair to become an agricultural county of no mean importance. There are several streams, the Uranos, the La Plata, the Animas, the Florida and the Los Piños, in the county, capable of irrigating the 70,000 acres of arable land which it contains. The elevation is only 5,000 feet. The climate admits of the maturing of melons, sugar-cane, tomatoes and fruits, and stock roams on the ranges the year round without shelter or prepared food. There is room for a large number of farmers.

TOWNS AND CAMPS.

Del Norte, 285 miles southwest of Denver and 30 miles from Alamosa (on the Denver & Rio Grande Railway), is the general supply point for the mines of Summit district, as well as of San Luis Valley, at the southern edge of which it is located. Its altitude is 7,750 feet, contains about 1,000 inhabitants, and is connected with Alamosa by daily stage. Lake City, 364 miles southwest of Denver, via Alamosa and Del Norte, or 285 miles from Denver via the Denver, South Park & Pacific Railway and Gunnison City, is the metropolis of northern San Juan. It contains some 1,100 inhabitants, two weekly papers, one of which, the *Silver World*, has a reputation throughout the country as one of the best mining journals in Colorado, and two extensive smelting establishments. Its altitude is 8,550 feet. Ouray, 300 miles southwest of Denver, via the Gunnison City route, contains about 900 inhabitants, and supplies the Mount Sneffles, San Miguel and adjacent regions. Altitude, 7,640 feet. Silverton, 390 miles southwest of Denver, via the Denver & Rio Grande Railway, is beautifully situated on the Animas River, and is the supply point for all the rich mining camps near the head of that stream described in this article. Its population is 800, and altitude 9,400 feet. Durango, it is generally believed, will be the metropolis of the San Juan country. Its population is about 2,000, and rapidly increasing. Coking ovens, smelting works, and a good class of buildings are going up. It is reached via the Denver & Rio Grande Railway (which will be completed to the town during the summer of 1881) and the Sanderson Stage Line. It is 390 miles southwest of Denver, and has an altitude of 6,800 feet. Rico, 45 miles northwest of Durango, as already noted, is queen of the new carbonate fields, and contains some 1,100 souls. It is best reached via Durango. All of these points are now easily reached from the Missouri river via the Kansas Pacific Railway from Kansas City or Leavenworth, or via the Union Pacific Railway from Omaha.

AS TO THE FUTURE.

The San Juan country will in two years be penetrated from end to end by at least two lines of railway. It contains every element desired to build up several of the richest mining communities in the world, and has only lacked this advance of the iron horse. Its climate, though rigorous, can not prevent underground operations the year round. Its smelting facilities of fuel, lime, water, and all varieties and grades of ore, are unexcelled. To say that some of the largest smelting works in the world will now soon spring up in the San Juan mountains, and that they will turn out millions of dollars where thousands are found now, is entirely reasonable. That thousands of poor prospectors will in this great wilderness yet "strike it rich," and that thousands of capitalists will by making judicious investments reap still greater rewards, is in such a country simply inevitable. The time will soon come when Gunnison and San Juan will be regarded as the bulwarks of the mining industry not only of Colorado, but of the whole southwest. It now only remains for us to see who will be the fortunate participants in the work which will attain this gratifying end.

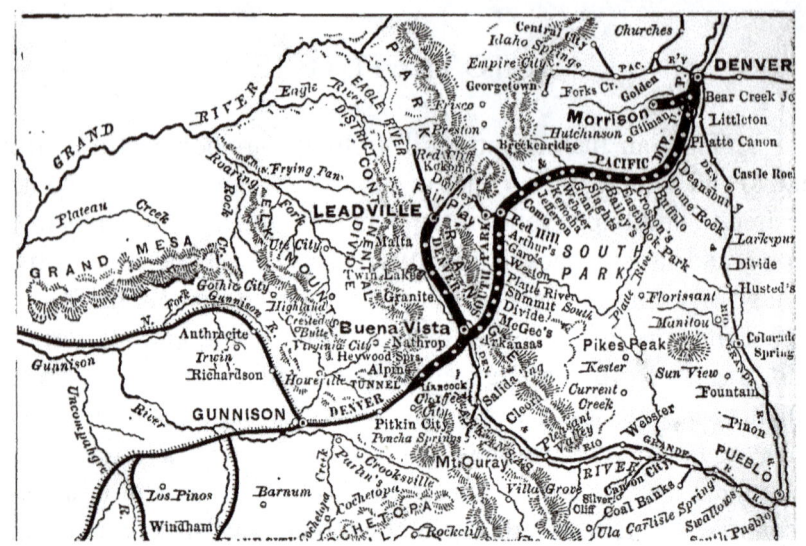

SYNOPSIS OF MINING LAWS—1880

Only citizens, and those who have declared their intention to become such, can legally locate mines.

All land is mineral that is more valuable for mining than farming purposes.

In Colorado the size of lode claims is not uniform in all counties, being in the older counties of Gilpin, Clear Creek, Boulder and Summit 1,500 by 150, and in others 1,500 by 300 feet.

The location of fissure veins, to be valid, must be upon the vein, and the side line must be equi-distant from the centre of the vein.

If at any point along the side lines the vein departs from the surface boundaries, the location beyond such point is defeasible, if not void. By the dip of the vein, that is its departure from the perpendicular in its downward course, the claimant may go outside of his side lines, provided that he has the top or apex of the vein within its boundaries.

The first requisite of a valid mining claim is the discovery of mineral "in place," and until that is done a claimant has no security in his possession. Mineral in place means where first deposited, as is distinguished from float, or such as has been detached from its native place. The latter can be made the basis of a placer claim only.

Discovery alone gives title for the time allowed by law for the completion of location and record, and after location and record have been made the title still relates back to the time of discovery.

A neglect to do the annual labor, as required by law, leaves a claim open to relocation. But any neglect to do the annual labor does not work a forfeiture of the claim, unless after such neglect and before the original locator has resumed work, another has located the claim and after re-entry of the first locator, the title relates back to their first location.

The law says that not "less than $100 worth of labor be performed or improvements made during each year," and the general interpretation has been that the annual period dates from the time of the location, but it has been decided recently by the Land Department that the assessment work is to be done during the calender year, that is, from January to January.

The discoverer must record within 20 days from the date of the discovery, and his location certificate must contain: (1) the name of the vein; (2) the same of the locator; (3) the date of location; (4) the number of feet in length claimed on each side of the discovery shaft; (5) the number of feet in width claimed on each side; (6) the general course of the vein, as near as may be.

The discovery shaft must show a well defined vein; a plain notice embracing the above facts must be posted at the point of discovery. The surface boundaries must be marked by eight substantial posts, (besides discovery) hewed on the sides facing the location, and sunk in the ground or firmly planted in monuments of stone, and are arranged as shown in the following diagram:

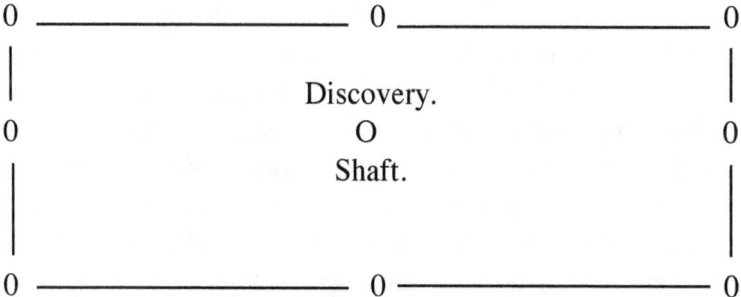

Any cut deep enough to disclose the vein, or a 10-foot adit or trench along the vein from the point of discovery, would be a legal discovery shaft.

The discover has 30 days from the time of uncovering a vein to sink his discovery shaft. (Locators cannot exercise too much care in defining their veins at the outset.)

In order to hold a vein before the patent issues, work must be done or improvements made to the value of $100 a year; and within six months from the year within which outlay is required to be made, the person who made such outlay, or some person for him, shall make and record an affidavit of the fact, and the recorder's certificate shall be prima facie evidence of the performance of such labor or the making of such improvements.

The relocation of abandoned claims shall be by erecting new boundaries, and by sinking a new discovery shaft, or by sinking from the bottom of the old shaft as if it were a new shaft commenced from the surface. (The safer course is to sink a new shaft.)

When labor or improvements to the amount of $600 shall have been performed or made upon a vein, patent may be applied for.

Notice of such application must be published for 60 days, at the expiration of which time, if no adverse claim shall have been filed, it will be assumed that the applicant is entitled to a patent upon making the necessary proofs and paying the receiver of the district office the official fees and $5 per acre. The preliminaries of obtaining a patent are somewhat complex, and exactness is required in detail, whereof the applicant had better secure the services of an attorney who makes a specialty of such business.

Placer mining claims may be patented at $2.50 per acre, or at that rate of fractional parts of an acre, under like circumstances and conditions, and upon similar proceedings, as are provided for veins; but no placer location can embrace more than 20 acres for each individual claimant, or more than 460 acres in one application.

A patent for a placer claim conveys any vein embraced which was not known to exist when the patent was applied for; but when a mineral vein is known to be embraced in the placer tract at the time of making application the fact must be distinctly stated, when the patent will issue including such vein upon the applicant paying $5 per acre therefor, including 25 feet of surface ground on each side thereof.

Owners of quartz-mills and reduction works, as well as quartz-mine claimants, can claim not to exceed five acres of non-mineral land for a mill site, upon making the required proofs, and paying $5 per acre therefor.

Mill sites may be applied for along with applications for mines with which they may be connected.

Water rights for mining purposes vest by priority of possession, and all patents granted are subject to vested rights.

No location of a mining claim shall be made until the discovery of a vein or lode within the limits of the claim located.

The locators, so long as they comply with the laws, and State, Territorial and local regulations, have the exclusive right of possession and enjoyment of all the surface included within the lines of their locations, and of all veins, lodes and ledges throughout their entire depth, the top or apex of which lies inside of such surface lines extended downward vertically, although such veins, lodes or ledges may so far depart from a perpendicular in their course downward as to extend outside the vertical side-lines of said surface locations; provided that their right of possession to such outside parts of such veins or ledges shall be confined to such portions thereof as lie between vertical planes drawn downward through the end-lines of their locations, so continued in their own direction that they will intersect such exterior parts of said veins or ledges.

Where a vein or lode is known to exist within the boundaries of a placer claim, an application for a patent, which does not include an application for the vein or lode claim, is construed as a conclusive declaration that the claimant of the placer claim has no right of possession of the vein or lode claim; but where the existence of a vein or lode in a placer claim is not known, a patent for the latter includes all valuable mineral or ore deposit within the boundaries thereof.

Where two or more veins intersect, priority of title governs, and the prior location is entitled to all ore or mineral contained within the space of intersection.

Where a tunnel is run for the development of a vein or lode, or for the discovery of mines, the owner of such tunnel has the right of possession of all veins or lodes within 3,000 feet from the face of such tunnel or the line thereof, not previously known to exist and discovered in the tunnel, to the same extent as if discovered from the surface; and locations, on the line of such a tunnel, of veins or lodes not appearing on the surface, made by other parties after the commencement of the tunnel, and while the same is being prosecuted with reasonable diligence, are invalid.

Any three miners, in a part of the country which has not been districted, can form a mining district, and make such laws as the circumstances of the mineral and the district require. They can enact that the size of claims, located after the formation of the district, shall be less than 600 by 1,500 feet, but they cannot reduce the width to less than 25 feet, nor can they alter the size of claims located prior to the formation of the district. When they form, they place on file in the county recorder's office, a description of the territory intended to be included in the district.

The question as to whether the same man may take up more than one claim on the same vein is an unsettled one, and different views are held. As a matter of fact, men do take more than one claim on the same lode and hold them. In New Mexico, Chief Justice Prince has decided, in the First Judicial District, which includes the northern half of that Territory, that one man cannot take more than one claim on the same vein; but that he can take one on each new vein that he discovers, and in that way he can have as many claims as he finds veins. The Supreme Court of the Territory has not yet been asked to pass on the question, and neither, of course, has the Supreme Court of the United States, so that the question is still undecided. In the Second and Third districts of New Mexico, the southern half of the Territory, the question has never been ruled on, and there men take as many extensions as they can perform their assessment work on.

ROUTES TO GUNNISON.

Gunnison is as easily reached as was Leadville a year ago, and railroads are approaching so rapidly that the travel of 1881 will mainly come by rail. From the Eastern seaboard to the Missouri river in these days of elaborate railway advertising, the route is plain, and thence to Denver one cannot well go amiss. If the traveler reaches the Missouri at Kansas City or Leavenworth he takes the old KANSAS PACIFIC LINE; if he comes by the more northerly belt and lands at Omaha, the UNION PACIFIC is the open sesame. By either of these routes he comes from the Missouri river to Denver in about thirty-one hours, there connecting with trains of either the Denver, South Park and Pacific, or Denver and Rio Grande railways, he journeys through some of Colorado's grandest scenery some ten hours to those common points, Alpine (present terminus D., S.P. & P. Railway), and Poncha Springs (on the D.&R. G. Railway), from where Concord coaches of the Sanderson line convey him through to Gunnison City in ten hours. Time from either Kansas City, Leavenworth or Omaha to Gunnison, about fifty-one hours.

Index

Abbey, C. F. – 53
Adams, General Charles – 8
Agriculture – 12, 56-61
Alabama Mine – 23
Alamosa (town) - 78
Allerton, Samuel – 40
Alpine Mountain – 10, 48
Alpine Pass – 48
Alvord, C. C. – 75
American Smelting Company – 43
Animas City – 71
Anna Dietrick Mine – 52
Animas Forks (town) – 72
Animas River – 72, 73, 78
Anthracite Coal – 14, 15, 23-25, 58
Anthracite Creek –14, 21, 24
Armstrong Gulch – 50
Ashcraft District – 54
Ashtabula Mine – 72
Aspen (town) – 53, 55, 56
Aspen Mine – 73
Avery, T. M. – 40

Baker's Park – 72
Bank of Gunnison – 14, 65
Banking – 64
Baxter Lode – 32

Belle of the West Mine – 71
Belle of Titusville Mine – 43
Belsey Mine – 42
Bent's Old Fort – 5
Bertha Mine – 50, 76
Boston Mine – 72
Boucher, C. S. – 17
Brennon, Jim – 8
Brittle Silver Mine – 23, 52
Broad Gauge Mine – 42,
Buck, E. A. – 17
Buddee, L. – 43
Bullion King Mine – 13, 15, 17, 26, 56, 60
Burn's Gulch – 72
Business – 64

California Gulch – 6, 7, 72
Camp Willard – 47, 57, 59
Capitalists, Advice to – 26, 27, 57, 58, 63
Castle Creek – 54
Castle Peak – 11
Catapult Mine – 41
Cement Creek – 13, 35
Cement Creek Mining District – 44
Cement Creek Springs – 34, 35
Cherry, Jas. A. – 72

Chicago Park – 52
Chloride King Mine – 51, 53, 55
Cleveland Mine – 73
Climate – 59, 60
Coal – 33, 34, 77
Coal Creek – 32, 33
Coal Creek Valley – 30
Cochetopa Creek – 12, 46, 47
Cochetopa Mineral Belt – 47
Cochetopa Pass – 5
Colorado State Mine – 31
Comstock, Thomas B. – 73
Copper Creek – 13, 38, 44
Cora Estelle Mine – 44
Cost of Living – 28, 66, 67
Crested Butte – 9, 10, 13, 30-35
Crested Butte Smelter Works – 33
Crooke Smelter Works – 71
Crystal Mountain – 33, 42

Dead Man's Gulch – 6
Denver and Rio Grande Railroad – 3, 10, 20, 34, 67, 69, 73, 75, 78, 85
Denver, South Park and Pacific Railroad – 10, 24, 48, 67, 69, 85
Diablo Mine – 22
Doctor Mine – 44
Dodge, D. C. – 20
Dodson Mine – 50, 60
Dolores Carbonate Camp – 76
Dolores County – 75
Duncan, R. A. – 21
Durango (town) – 75, 77, 78

East River – 13, 33, 44
Eclipse Mine - 72
Elk Basin – 15, 23
Elk Mine – 23
Elk Mountain Mines – 15-30
Elk Mountain Gold and Silver Co. – 31
Elk Mountain Range – 11, 33, 42, 68
Ella Mine – 22
Employment – 19, 21, 62, 66
Engineer Mountain – 71
Eureka (town) – 73
Eureka Mine – 22, 42

Fairview Mine – 13, 22, 49, 60
Fisher, W. A. – 18
Forest Queen Mine – 13, 15, 16, 18-22, 56, 57, 60
Fort Scott Mine – 52
Fossil Ridge – 53
Fremont, Charles – 6
Future of San Juan – 79

Gavitt Mine – 32
General Sales Lode – 22
Gilpin, Gov. William – 5
Glasgow Mine – 77
Gold Cup Mine –13, 53
Gold Hill – 50, 71
Gold Leaf Mine – 50
Golden Link Mine – 50
Golden Queen Mine – 70

Goodenough Milling & Mining – 27
Gothic (town) – 9, 18, 21, 42, 43, 44, 51, 56, 57, 58, 60, 64, 68
Grand Duchess Mine – 53
Grand River – 5, 7, 11, 42, 43
Grant, Judge – 34
Grant Park – 22
Great Western Mine – 41
Green and Company Smelter – 73
Greenleaf & Co. Concentrating – 72
Grey Copper Mine – 41
Gunnison, Capt. – 6
Gunnison (town) – 5, 8, 10, 14, 62, 63
Gunnison River – 5, 13,
Gunnison County/Country – 5-15, 56
Gunnison River/Valley – 9
Gypsy Mine – 31

Hack, John – 7
Hazelton Mountain – 72
Haverly, Jack – 14, 17, 41, 47, 64
Henson Creek – 71
Hidden Treasure Mine – 75
Highland Mine – 31, 32
High Tide Mine – 12
Highland Mary Mine – 72, 77
Hillerton Mining District – 9, 13, 53, 58
Holt, Col. W. T. – 20

Homestake Mine – 42
Hotchkiss Mine – 10, 71
Howard Extension Mine – 16, 17

Imogene Basin – 74, 75, 84
Independence Mine – 23, 58, 60
Indian Girl Mine – 41
Iowa Mining and Smelting Co. – 34
Inez Mine – 71
Iron deposits – 41
Irwin, Dick – 44
Irwin (town) – 13, 17, 18, 22, 24, 26, 28, 56-58, 60, 64, 68

Jacobson, Col. E. P. – 22
Jennings, John and David – 37, 38, 40
Justice Mine – 17

Kansas City Mine – 75
Kansas Pacific Railroad – 3, 10, 67, 78, 85
Kelley, Jim – 63
Kendall Mountain – 73
King Mine – 23
King Solomon Mountain – 73

Lake City (town) – 68, 71, 78
La Plata County – 77
Lake Fork of the Gunnison River – 71
Lake District – 70, 71
Lead Chief Mine – 21, 22, 26, 60
Lewiston Mine – 52
Little Annie Mine – 70, 77
Little Carry Mine – 52
Little Chief Mine – 21, 22
Little Per Cent Mine – 49, 51
Los Piños Agency – 8
Lots (City) – 17, 64
Lubricator Mine – 47
Luona Claim – 41, 42

Mace, O. P. – 18
Maid of the Mist Mine – 72
Mammoth Mine – 41, 42, 71
Maple Leaf Mine – 47
Marble – 32
Maroon Mountain – 13
Marshall Pass – 10, 48
Mastodon Mine – 72
Meeker massacre – 2, 9, 26
Mineral Farm Mine – 74
Miner's Delight Mine – 32
Mining Laws – 80-84
Mining Belt – 12
Monarch Mine – 53
Monte Christo Mine – 17
Mormons – 5, 6
Mother Shifton – 54
Mountain Queen Mine – 72

Needs of Gunnison County – 64, 65
New York World – 2, 4
Niagara Consolidated Mining and Reduction Co. – 73
Niagara Mountain – 74
North Star Mine – 73

Oh Be Joyful Gulch – 30, 31, 33
Ohio Creek – 14
Old Mexico deposit – 16
Old Sheik Mine – 13, 15 16, 17, 19
Ouray, Chief – 8
Ouray (town) – 73, 77

Palmer, General – 20
Palmetto Mine – 71
Park District – 71
Parlin's Ranch – 46
Parsons, Dr. John – 8
Peeler Basin – 30, 31
Picayune Gulch – 72
Pioneer Mine – 53
Pitkin (town) – 9, 45-47
Pitkin Mining District – 13, 48, 50, 51
Polar Star Mine – 72
Poland Mine – 23
Population – 68
Post Office, Irwin – 28, 29
Poughkeepsie Placer – 72

Poughkeepsie Gulch – 74
Pound Diggings – 6, 7, 47
Prospecting – 58

Quartz Creek – 9, 46, 48, 50

Rates of travel – 67, 68
Ranching – 12, 61, 77
Red Cloud Mine – 71
Red Cross Mine – 71
Red Well basin – 30, 31
Reduction of Ores – 27
Rentz's Gulch – 6
Richardson, Sylvester – 8
Rico (town) – 75-78
Rico Mining District – 75, 76
Roaring Fork River – 7, 11
Roaring Fork district – 53
Rock Creek – 7, 8, 25
Rock Creek District – 42, 43
Routes to Gunnison – 67, 85
Ruby Belt – 15, 16, 23
Ruby Camp – 13, 15, 23, 25, 26, 56
Ruby Chief Mine – 16, 23
Ruby King Mine – 13, 15, 18, 20
Ruby Silver Mining and Smelting Co. – 41
Ruby Mountain – 75

Saguache (town) – 8
San Juan – 69-79
San Luis Valley – 8, 78
Sands, Obadiah – 36, 37, 40
Schofield (town) – 43
Sherman, David H. – 37
San Miguel Creek – 75
San Miguel Mining District – 75
Silver Age – 49, 50
Silver Bell – 53, 54
Silver Islet Mine – 13, 49, 50
Silver Mountain – 38
Silverton – 72, 73, 78
Slaight, Nathaniel – 49
Slate River – 6, 30, 33-34
Smelting – 57, 58, 78
Smith, Howard F. – 34
Smuggler Mine – 53, 54, 75
Snow Blind Gulch – 6
Snow Mass Mountain – 11
Soule, W. L. G. – 28, 29
Spar Mine – 53, 54
Spring Creek – 13, 43
Sultan Mountain – 73
Summit Gold Mining District – 70, 78
Susquehanna Basin – 23
Susquehanna Mine – 73
Swedish Boy Mine – 54
Sylvanite Mine – 13, 36-40
Sylvanite Extension Mine – 41

Taylor, James – 7
Taylor Gulch – 7

Taylor Park – 6, 7
Taylor River – 7
Teocali Mountain – 11
Terror Mine – 43
Terrible Mine – 50, 57
Thompson, L. R. – 20
Thornburg massacre – 9, 26
Tincup Mining District – 13
Tinguely, Charles G. – 62
Tomichi (Tomitchi) River – 6, 9, 46, 52
Treasure Mountain – 13

Whopper Mine – 7, 8, 42
Whopper Mountain – 7, 13
Woodbury, R. W. – 20
Woerishoffer, Mr. – 20

Uncompahgre Mountain – 74
Uncompahgre River – 5, 11, 74
Union Park – 6
Union Pacific Railroad – 67
Ute Indians – 14, 26
Ute-Ule Mine – 71

Valleys – 61, 62
Virginia Mine – 41
Virginius Mine – 74, 75

Wages – 28, 56, 59, 66
Waite, George and Lewis – 7, 8, 42
Warren, Ira D. – 37
Washington Gulch – 6, 7, 30-32
Wheeler & Kimball Placer Claim – 75

www.ingramcontent.com/pod-product-compliance
Lightning Source LLC
Chambersburg PA
CBHW070654050426
42451CB00008B/344